Grandparents
Talk

Grandparents *Talk*

Janice Marriott

Bateman

To Dr David Pendergrast and his team at
Greenlane Eye Hospital, and Sarah Hunt
of Hunt and Gaunt, without whom nothing at
all would have been possible, and with whose
skills a new world has been made visible for me.

Text © Janice Marriott 2016

Published in 2016 by David Bateman Ltd
30 Tarndale Grove, Albany, Auckland, New Zealand

www.batemanpublishing.co.nz

A catalogue record for this book is available from the National Library of New Zealand.

ISBN 978-1-86953-948-1

Publisher: Bill Honeybone
Book design: Cheryl Smith
All internal photographs by the author unless specified.
Printed in China through Colorcraft Ltd, Hong Kong

Contents

Eclipsed

Sometimes, child, I feel as battered as the moon
And as cold, as alone, and as old.
Always in orbit, turning,
My face towards yours, yearning,
You, my Earth, core of my gravity.

Sometimes I am Saturn
And you run rings round me.
Sometimes you are angry red Mars
And I take so long to reach you
And stumble when I get there.

Mostly you are the sun,
And when we build towers or hunt tigers
For hours and hours, or roll gingerbread,
I warm my cold, old, battered self
In your burning, burning brightness.

Please, when it's bedtime, don't howl at me.
I am doing my best, pretending to be
A Sea of Tranquility.
Goodnight, sleep tight, my little star.
How I wonder what you really are.

Introduction

❦

The urge to write a book about grandparents came to me when I was looking at sculptures on the Te Atatu Sculpture Walk. A friend was reading to me words by Kate Spence associated with Anton Forde's sculptures: 'Our kuia know to protect our children. Our kuia know to keep our children fed, warm and sheltered. Our kuia know to protect our whenua. Our kuia know …' A girl, maybe three years old, and a woman, maybe 60, were listening, the grandmother with her hand on the girl's shoulder. I noticed that the girl's ponytail was pulled through a hole in the top of her sun hat. This made me smile at the grandmother, and she understood my smile. She told me the hole was her way of keeping the girl's hat on.

Just an ordinary interaction on a hot day, but its ordinariness seemed to me so extraordinary: the practicality of the grandmother, the shared love — conveyed by that hand on her granddaughter's shoulder — and we two grandmothers acknowledging each other. Is something that ordinary the glue that keeps families and even communities functioning? And what is that glue made of? Continuity? Trust? Love? Probably all of those, and more.

I set out to explore more of these extraordinary ordinary moments. I chose to do this by interviewing, face-to-face, a variety of grandparents. None would think they were extraordinary, but they all were. I knew few of them before I interviewed them. I listened carefully and felt the bond that all of them had with their grandchildren.

You don't plan to become a grandparent. It is out of your control. It is a role often doomed to heartbreak, because the grandparent usually ends up loving the child far more than the child loves them in return.

It is about giving rather than receiving, as Shewaynesh says, and it is about accepting that your children and your children's partners are in control of the practices and values surrounding the upbringing of your grandchildren. You are in the back seat. You are not the driver. For some grandparents that isn't easy.

Parents work to earn the money for the family. The most recent census, that of 2013, tells us that 40.3 per cent of mothers with dependent children were employed full-time. Someone is looking after those children when the parents are at work. Often that person is a grandparent. A grandparent's unpaid childcare may be enabling the parents to pay a mortgage or their rent. Polly describes how she helps in this way. Many grandparents, including Polly, also work and, like Isabelle Isaako, have to make hard decisions about how to fit work and nurturing into already packed lives. Because most grandparents do not feature in the formal statistics and have informal childcare arrangements, well under the radar of the IRD, Child, Youth and Family (CYF) or the census, the exact workload of grandparents within a family structure is unknown.

We do know that the number of grandparents who take on full responsibility for raising their grandchildren is increasing. That 2013 census tells us there were 9543 grandparents doing this. The major cause of children not living with their parents is drug and alcohol problems affecting the parents. Thank goodness for Di Vivian and the organisation she started, Grandparents Raising Grandchildren, which advocates on behalf of these grandparents.

In 2010, the Families Commission published a report about grandparenting, *Changing Roles*. Nothing like this survey has been done since. Over 57 per cent of those surveyed saw a grandchild at least once a week. For grandparents under 55 years of age, about 41 per cent looked after grandchildren on a regular basis; 48 per cent said they sometimes put their own interests and needs on hold to look after grandchildren; 95 per cent of those surveyed said looking after their grandchildren was enjoyable.

In the report it states the obvious: 'It is clear that grandparents play a significant role in the lives of many New Zealand families, providing support across a wide range of areas. In particular, the provision of both regular and irregular childcare is of considerable assistance, helping parents to remain in the labour market as well as allowing them time for other activities such as study, or a break from the demands of family life. Financial contributions, small and large, are another way in which some grandparents are supporting their grandchildren and their families, even though this can lead to their own finances being stretched.'

I realised that, regardless of whether my interviewees were retired or not, none were solely grandparents. They have lives rich with complex achievements and skills as well. I discovered how both Stacey Naish's and Di Menefy's nursing skills have come in handy when grandparenting. Wylie built and flew his own plane, and now at last he has a grandson to build go-karts for. Ro is a cake decorator, and keeps Ben engaged with icing, like tasty play-dough, while she works. Teachers, like Marion, McGregor and Leautuli, never seem to stop teaching. Those who are coaches end up coaching the whole school, or the club their grandchild is involved in, like Colin and Charles. Builders, like John, modify their houses for the extended family. Te Maari and Vera make sure their houses have one big room where the whole whanau can gather.

Some pass down talents, like Polly, Te Maari or Kate, or instil values, like Rosemary. Some, like Isabella, want to teach their grandchildren how to save money. Faiza, Awthash, Te Maari and Piripi pass on cultural knowledge and language. Penny and Stacey have family businesses their grandchildren might or might not join. Some grandchildren follow in a grandparent's footsteps — or stirrups, in the case of Graham's granddaughters.

There is no such thing as a standard nuclear family anymore. As Toby, Paula's son, says: 'So few children at school live with their original parents.' There are extended families, like Di and John Conway's, reconstituted families, like Glenda and Phil's, adopted grandchildren, like Shona's, and gay families, like McGregor and Russell, and Annie and Jo.

Some people's grandchildren all live, unexpectedly, close by — how lucky for well-travelled people like Penny, Yolande and Keng Mow Chen — but so many people have grandchildren overseas. For them it is long-distance love. Christine went across the world to live with her grandchildren. For Sue and Wylie, Marietjie, and the Hebleys, Skype or FaceTime have become their communication medium, and gift-wrapped Hairy Maclary books and merino sleeping bags for babies are constantly flying across the world.

Pat and Joan, who have both experienced deaths of children, and Di Menefy, whose daughter-in-law died leaving two sons, mention the importance of touching in families, as do Shewaynesh and Isabelle; and touch is what all the Skypers miss so much. 'Keeping in touch by Skype' is an ironic phrase.

Many interviewees, like Joan and Te Maari, pondered the difference between their role as grandparents and that of their own grandparents. Most, like Stacey and Wylie, thought about how best to protect and prepare their grandchildren for an uncertain future. Most worried about global warming and the increasing gulf between the haves and the have-nots, none more actively than Rosemary. Within 30 years there could be unpredictable climate, insufficient food, wars and/or there could be colonies on Mars and the moon. Within a century there could be a generation of space-bred babies who could live off-Earth, never ever going 'home'. We do not know.

Some grandparents live with teenage grandchildren, like Leautuli does. Many grandparents imagine, like Annie, that they will be ports in the storm when their toddler grandchildren are teenagers. These grandparents often don't realise that they will also be 10 years older, frailer, tireder. Maybe it is a feature of grandparents to *not* accept that they are aging at the same rate their grandchildren are.

In these interviews you won't read solely about the joys of grandparenting. Often grandparenting involves sacrifice and struggle. Grandparents can be rocks for their grandchildren to cling to when marriages fail, like the Burketts are, but it's possible, too, for grandparents to lose their grandchildren completely in the shake-up and rearrangement of their children's lives.

I was moved by the commitment of couples like the Pritchards and the Suttons, when helping grandchildren with special needs. I was astounded and moved by the heroic efforts of Ro, raising an autistic great-grandchild as well as a grandchild. I imagine the constant tiredness and the dedication.

Plenty of grandparents raise grandchildren on their own, like Isabelle and Marion. I saw the fierceness and doggedness of them both, and of Di Vivian, all of whom battled for custody of their grandchildren in order to give them a chance. Di has shared her experiences and helped thousands of other grandparents by founding Grandparents Raising Grandchildren, through which she has fought to get an allowance for these grandparents equivalent to that of foster carers. I applaud her and her organisation.

And I also salute those interviewees, like Annie, Stuart, Vera and Yolande, who wanted to talk, and talk, about their delight in discovering the wonder of having and playing with a grandchild. Talking to all of them has been a privilege.

Science tells us that by helping our children raise their children we are securing our genes in another generation. It's just the genes driving us, they say. Hmm. We all think it is a lot more than that. It's love, pure and simple. Of course we lose the intensity of the relationship as the grandchildren grow. They crack open that fragile shell of our love and escape, as independent as newly-hatched crocodiles, into a new world that doesn't care about grandparents at all. It is their world, not ours. Ah, life is tough for us. But it doesn't stop us from adoring them, treasuring their every moment, the times when we feel we have cheated old age, been born again, and have a foothold on the rock of immortality.

Photo by Mia Fitzgerald

Me and my grandson, Tane

Living stories

My grandson, Tane, is now four and eleven-twelfths years old. I have looked after him during these years while his parents work. Looking after Tane is like looking after my garden; it requires constant attention and many little interventions, the sort no one else notices. All that will soon, unfortunately, stop. Why? I have to hand care of this precious being over to the state. The school uniform has already been bought.

The main activity we have shared in his preschool life is re-enactments of myth and story. When he was two, I told him about the three little pigs and their house-building. While I then made his dinner, he busied himself in the garden. I couldn't see what he was doing, just that he was running to and fro. When I checked, he had made three piles — one of grass, one of wood and one of bricks. Oh, what a moment for me! But I nearly spoilt it when I tried to remove the teetering piece of brick from the top of the brick house. 'No,' said the angry child. 'That important. That the chimney!' Of course. There would be no satisfactory ending without that chimney for the wolf to fall down, would there? I realised then how meaningful stories were to him, in all their essential detail.

Since then, many stories have lived in us. Here are just a few.

In the pouring rain, we huddled undercover in the courtyard and I told him about Noah's Ark. I went inside to make lunch, and he stayed there and built a raft out of wood, with a gangplank, He showed me this. 'See? He loading the ark now, two by two. Two Toyotas, two diggers, two fire engines, two ambulances, two forklifts.'

'Right. What's that rescue helicopter doing on the deck?'

'That go out to find the olive branch. *Tucka tucka tucka tucka.*'

'Gotcha.'

Now we dive into Grimms' fairy tales and Greek myths. We build the stories up together, ideas for each new plot pulse coming from either him or me. He rarely accepts my ideas. I always accept his. Thus the gifts the baby Sleeping Beauty receives might be lifelong diesel or a CAT digger, rather than goodness and the power to dance. Rapunzel may clear the prickly forest away with her own feller buncher, and cure her beloved's blindness with the judicious application of Grandma's eye drops. Snow White's coffin will be on a wide-load truck going down Mt Eden Road with flashing lights and perhaps a siren.

Sometimes the stories end abruptly before they've begun. I am telling him *Jack and the Beanstalk*. 'Jack and his mum were so hungry they had nothing to eat—'

'Look! Here comes Fireman Sam, and he's brought food for us!' End of story.

Or we do get the story acted out, up to the part where the giant is chasing Jack in the castle. We are rushing through my garden, acting this out. I have almost caught Jack, but he phones the police for help and my character is promptly arrested and that is the end of that.

Famous disasters also fuel Tane's imaginary world. We build Tacoma bridges and shake small cars off them until the bridge crashes satisfactorily. We re-enact the *Hindenburg* fire with all of our fire trucks, and with the papier-mâché *Hindenburg* I made using drink bottles for the armature, which has lasted, used every day, for two years now. We have a papier-mâché Vesuvius, too, which occasionally explodes red wool, red streamers and pumice stones. I am often a skeleton being exhumed by an archaeologist in Pompeii, after the magic words 'Time passed.' Thomas the Tank Engine and carriages are commandeered to be the Tangiwai train. *Titanic*, surrounded by bubbles rather than ice, sinks over and over again in my claw-foot bath. I don't know why disasters are so appealing, and I presume they won't always be, but while they feed his inner world I provide the basic stimulus — the books, the story-telling. He's trying to understand the concept of past and future, but I'm in the present, knowing how fleeting it is and how fallible my memory of it will become. He feasts on the equally magical worlds of myth and history, while I'm satisfied more simply by his wide-open wonder-filled eyes.

We never read the actual words in picture books. We make up our own, more exciting, ones. We avoid books that show grandmothers with aprons, grey hair, and looking for their glasses. We tried reading chapter books, but stopped when Tane threw *George's Marvellous Medicine* into the rubbish bin; it was the strongest statement he could make to show his disgust at how Roald Dahl portrayed a grandmother. We have learnt that books can be more dangerous than disasters.

We have had our share of real near-disasters. I discovered that Tane, transformed into a high-speed Ghan train chuffing through the Australian desert around Mt Eden's crater rim, could go off on a siding and disappear. It is that sickness in the throat, that banging in the chest, that breathlessness, the tight ache in the legs, the spinning and seething brain turned into a cauldron — all that — that tells us what our grandchildren are to us, and how vulnerable they make us. If anything should happen … Ten minutes later we were reunited, and Tane was telling me fiercely he wasn't lost. 'I changed into the Santa Fe freight train crossing America. I was nearly at Chicago.'

Strangely, I don't write any of these moments down. I have no Tane diary. After handing over control at the end of my shift, I step into my own world; I don't want to spend my time writing up Tane's. Grandparents have other lives, too. The art is to have the two high-speed trains chugging along in sight of each other.

♡

I Love Staying at nan and grandads house at the weekend. We watch funny movies and eat popcorn. We have a pillow fight and grandad always loses. We have Some dancing time that i Love. We do arts and crafts with my granan. I Love Saturday nights!! ♥

Stuart and Shona Fraser

❧∾❧

Saturday night

'On Saturdays we finish work at 12 noon at our hairdressing salon. Every second Saturday, we go to Stacey's, our daughter's. And every other Saturday we all gather at our house. The family weekend starts usually at three o'clock with a big family dinner, then Harmony, our granddaughter, comes back to us and her parents go off. She's six. Our precious weekend time with her begins with music, very loud music. In the car on the journey back to our house, she always asks for a rock station, so she gets a rock station. She sits in the back of the car, head swinging, doing car dancing. We all slap our legs and we all take turns singing a song. When we get home, we greet Shona's mother, Peggy, who came out from Scotland to be with us when her husband died. She lives with us. She's 83. Harmony always gives her a flying hug. "GranNan!" she yells. Greeting over, our special weekend time gears up. We move all the furniture. We put MTV on up loud and we dance and dance.

'GranNan doesn't sit on the sidelines and watch. She's in amongst it, dancing, too. Peggy goes to gym on Mondays and Thursdays. She walks everywhere. She's fit. Harmony dresses her up, even makes her up. Shona walked into Peggy's bedroom one Saturday and there, under a mound of blankets on the floor, was GranNan. There were even hats on top of the pyramid. And Harmony said, "Where's GranNan? Anyone seen GranNan?" We said, "You can't do that to your great-grandmother." But Peggy loves it. They both love it. We bought Harmony a mic and she has a wee amplifier, and all of a sudden you might hear her, through the speakers, announcing "Here's *GranNan's Show*, the fashion show", and GranNan will walk into the room with a tiara on, nails painted, lipstick on. Again, we say, "You can't do that to your GranNan", but GranNan says she likes it.

'Our grandchildren's job is to try to break my body. I'm the horse, the dance partner. Harmony's a drama queen. She'll do a dance, then she'll go "Taa-daaa!" and say, "You can clap now." The dancing lasts about half an hour, then we get the popcorn out and the hot pepperoni salami. That's the food Harmony loves. And then we have a pillow-fight. You never know it's going to happen — until Harmony comes screaming at you with a pillow. Seven or eight times my glasses have broken during a pillow-fight. I remember now to wear my fighting-with-the-kids glasses on Saturday nights. We then calm down a bit and have movie-time — her choice of movie. So it might be *Frozen*, or *Strange Magic* is the one at the moment. Then it's ice cream, grapes, oh and more popcorn. She also likes broccoli, and she loves strawberry milk. Because she loves strawberries so much, I always gives her strawberry things for Christmas — plates, sugar bowls, milk jugs. She's starting a collection.

'Last weekend, because my mother was waiting for a new bed to

Harmony and Tyler

be delivered, and she was temporarily using Harmony's mattress, we all decided to have a sleepover on mattresses in the lounge. Usually everyone falls asleep during or after the movie. It's GranNan first, then me [Stuart], then there's just Shona and Harmony. Sometimes they watch the movie twice. Then Shona pops Harmony into bed. End of Saturday night at home.

'Another grandchild, Ryan, lives up the coast with his mother, so we don't see so much of him, but when Ryan and Harmony are both staying here together we always make up a bed in the lounge for them and they sleep there on movie nights. Ryan wanted to buy a movie for Harmony for her birthday this year, because that's what they do at Grandad's house. Our house is where they do all this fun stuff.

'What else would we be going to do on a Saturday night? You might stay home and watch a horror movie, and wake up in the morning frantic and your head all stuffed up because you've been watching blood and guts all Saturday night, but not us. We watch kids' cartoons, and we wake on Sunday and our psyche is all quietened and cleaned out.'

Sunday morning, Shona gets up and goes for a run, but Peggy (GranNan) and Stuart make a cooked breakfast for themselves. Stuart loves cooking, so in go potato scones, sausages, bacon, eggs, beans. Harmony has none of that. She likes toast and jam and butter, and it has to be cut the right way, with no crusts. Even though she eats sliced strawberries all summer, she picks the fruit out of the strawberry jam before spreading it on her toast. Shona is the only one who can make the toast right for Harmony. She has to be back from her run in time to do it.

GranNan always looks at her breakfast and says, 'I always look forward to this Sunday breakfast. I never know where to start.'

'She's been saying that every Sunday for three years,' said Stuart. 'If Harmony is still hungry, she wants ice cream. We think she's a really good eater during the week at home, but at our place she can be spoiled, and she can eat what she wants. We don't have to buy the socks, shoes, vests, etc., anymore. We just buy the treats.

'After breakfast on Sunday morning, we take her swimming. We all sit there like the Munsters — GranNan, us, my daughter, her husband — in a row, watching Harmony in the pool. So that's our Saturday night, Sunday morning from go to whoa. It will all change, of course, when her brand-new brother, baby Tyler, is older. Saturday nights themselves can't change; they'll just involve more kids.

'Grandchildren keep you happy. They make you laugh.'

'It doesn't matter how horrible you might be feeling about something, if Harmony wanders into the room with her massive smile, her ability to communicate with you like no other kid would, well, she sets the whole world to rights. We have such pride in her. It started when she was really small. She didn't walk. She always ran. She couldn't stop running. At the moment, she thinks I have magic powers. She thinks I have magic in my hands because I can take splinters out. But, like someone said, "One day I'll come down from the hill and they'll know I'm just a man."

'We are trying to make the grandkids think that our house is home. Any one of the family can come anytime. They all have their own homes now, but there is always a place for anyone here if they need it. They don't need to ask.'

When Stacey and Rick and Harmony were moving house and had a six months' wait for the house they were moving into, they stayed in Stuart and Shona's house for that time. They all helped to rearrange the place to fit.

'We don't mean that our house is the centre of the family. It is just one family house. If we tried to make it the centre, it would be as though we thought their houses were just toy houses, and that's not what we are meaning it to be. Harmony has her own room in our house. She loves coming here. She owns the place. She doesn't like sharing us. We are all her slaves.

'We maintain a relationship with Ryan's mum, Michelle, even though that marriage has broken up. So many couples break up now, and grandparents often lose their grandchildren in the separation. Especially the son's parents often end up being kept away from the grandchildren. We've never wanted that to happen. I hope the pillow-fights can teach the grandkids something. They learn here that a little tap grows to a big fight that can end up with Grandad on the floor with broken glasses. They learn when it has to stop. It's like that with the parents' relationships. Little snipes can grow and break you. It's our job to make sure that doesn't happen. You have to be involved, all the time, to be able to help. It's a tribal thing. When the parents' relationship falls apart, we feel it isn't just their failure. It is ours as well, because we are supposed to be the glue that keeps the family together. You have to work at it.

'I come from a broken family,' said Stuart, 'so I feel that you have to make sure that all these links stay together. I need to make sure the parents are happy and being good to each other. It's a grandparent's job. You can see they might be having difficulties, but you can also see that they are just tired and need a break. I look at Harmony and baby Tyler and I think they won't ever be a problem, because we will make it work. We won't make Harmony feel that we have less love to give her because we have to give some to her new brother. No. He will work his way into our hearts. We'll create a new bond with him. We'll have more love to give.

'We don't say, "They are my grandkids, so I'm going to adore them unconditionally." That's rubbish. You don't want a kid who just sits there and screams. You set standards and boundaries. You work at it. If they misbehave, you make them know what isn't going to work at your place. We used to have this naughty corner thing if Harmony had been cheeky, and at first she wouldn't go there, so I went and sat there and she didn't like that. She got upset and dragged me out of there. After that, she always behaves. It wasn't punishing her; it was showing her. If you annoy me, I come out and bite. It's the Glaswegian in me. Harmony has good-behaviour stickers on her wall, and crosses if she's naughty. She has to be twice as good to earn a sticker to cover up a cross.

'Grandparents can be naughty, too. When we had our kids we were young, and we never got to have the fun we are having now. Now we like to buy Harmony noisy things; things that will cause trouble when she takes them home.

'Because my son, Pete, and his partner have split, and he's now in Whitianga, whereas his son Ryan is up north, it's hard to get together for family occasions, such as Father's Day, for example. But Father's Day is all about being there for your children; if Peter can't be with Ryan on Father's Day, then Ryan is with me. A grandfather is just a step up from a father. You have to fill in for your son at the times he can't do his share of the parenting after a separation. Father's Day isn't about you being pampered. It's about you being available. I tell my son and son-in-law this. Same with Mother's Day.

'We work full-time in the salon. I'm here very early each day, but, after work, well, what do you do after work? Come five o'clock, what are you going to do for the rest of the evening? Sit at a table and eat your dinner! If the grandkids need us to go and do something, well, we do it. If Stacey needs us to take Harmony — like, when she was pregnant and heavy with Tyler, we took Harmony for the school holidays. If you put that amount of energy in, you get the benefits later. Now that Tyler's been born, we need to look after Stacey's mental wellbeing. She's exhausted with Tyler. So we help, because everyone's a winner then. Looking after our daughter is just as important as looking after Harmony and Tyler. It's all the same thing.

'Harmony loves having her hair cut. The last time she wasn't happy because we had to cut that much off because it was really ragged. She didn't like it, but when she got home she posed for all these photos of herself, waving her arms, standing on the coffee table.

'When we emigrated to New Zealand, we didn't have grandparents. It was just the two of us raising children. Especially when they got older, we were trying to guide them, but they were rejecting everything we were trying to teach them. If you have a grandparent there who can give the same message, but in a calmer way, that's good. They can just sit and talk to the kid. And then the kid often realises that they don't need to rebel, because they see the family as something long-term and stable. Most people live to 75 or more. How horrible to have no one before you or after you when you get to that age. You need a sense of a family line. I've made a big wooden box, and I'm going to fill it with family mementos, photos and things, treasures. And it's for all the grandchildren to look at. All kids need photographs of their ancestors. Harmony has only the one cousin on our side of the family, Ryan. But on her dad's Maori/Tongan side she has 24 cousins, so she has a huge sense of family.

'When Tyler was born I said, "My God, we are looking at someone who will probably be alive in the year 2100." I am going to live to be 205, because Stevie Wonder has a song called "Saturn". It's about how no one gets sick or goes to war and people live happily until 205.'

♡

Grandparents shouldn't have

- Textured or shagpile carpet — jigsaws, roads, building blocks, tall cranes won't stay flat on them.
- An overseas trip booked.
- Ming vases.
- A pitbull terrier.

Di Vivian

Fighting for grandparents

'We had three children of our own, and we took on two foster daughters when they were both 14. One of the foster children produced two children, and as a result of that my husband and I had children living in our house for 44 years before we were finally alone. Then we bought a convertible sports car. We toured around, buying antiques. Six months into this dream retirement we had a call from CYF saying they had uplifted the two daughters of our foster daughter. The two daughters were four and six. CYF asked us to take on these children. We struggled with that, because it wasn't an easy relationship with the mother. We decided we'd done our bit for society. It was our time now. But then one weekend we were asked if we could take the children just for the weekend to give the Barnardo's caregiver a break, so we took them, just for that weekend. We all went to a niece's ballet recital. We had a lovely time. I took them back to kindergarten and school on the Monday morning. That afternoon there was a knock on my door just after three, and there they were, the two little girls with two social workers who said they didn't have any beds for the children to go to. These little girls were just standing there, on the doorstep, looking in, while we were having this conversation. We couldn't say no. God had a plan for us, and it hadn't got anything to do with touring around the country in a convertible.

'From there, our life became what I can only describe as hell. The mother and the two different fathers phoned us all the time, threatening to kill us, accusing us of stealing their children. Then we got thrust into the Family Court, which we knew nothing about. We'd never been in court in our lives. We had to employ a Family Court lawyer. The children were placed in the care of CYF, but living with us for the next four years, and we had social workers coming and going to our house. We were involved in the Family Court every six months. It was daunting, and hugely costly. After four years we finally got the children under our care and protection, and CYF left us alone.

'I couldn't believe we were under such stress. I'm very organised. With my own children I was organised: 7am the crock-pot's on for dinner, I've got the babies and I'm ready to go off and play netball for the day. I'm that sort: but this was almost too much for me. I thought: am I the only person doing this kind of grandparenting? So, in 1999 I placed an ad in the *North Shore Times Advertiser* asking if there were any other grandparents in that situation, and would they like to get together. My phone has never stopped ringing. People are still ringing. At first I was up until 11pm answering calls. We held our first meeting, in Birkenhead. Ten grandparents turned up. We called ourselves Parenting Second Time Around, but as time went on we changed that to Grandparents Raising Grandchildren so that we'd be more focused on our actual role. I had been getting a lot of second marriages coming to us with stepchildren. That wasn't our focus. In 2002, we became a charitable trust and had a board. We now have over 6000 caregivers on our database and 43 support groups around the country, run by grandparents. We average 3000 calls a year to my home. If I had five cents for every tear that has been cried over that phone …

'We lobby government. We have employed a beneficiaries advocate to make sure grandparents are getting their entitlements. Two hundred and three dollars a week is the Unsupported Child Benefit for a 15-year-old. That's got to pay for food, sports, transport, clothes, iPads — the lot. A teenager can *eat* that in a week. We now have parity for the clothing allowance with foster carers. But I know it won't come in until 2018, and I know that what we fought for was a school-year start-up allowance, and the extraordinary care fund, and that will finish in 2018 — so government gives with one hand and takes with the other.

'Years ago we were offered a booth at the Seniors Expo in Greenlane. We decorated it to catch people's attention, and I hung a painting by one of my granddaughters on the wall at the back. It was in a balsa-wood frame. A man eyeballed me, hostile, and asked, "What did you do to your children to make them end up abusing their own children so you have to raise them?" I told him all of my children are pillars of society, except one who went off the rails on drugs and alcohol, and got involved with a violent man. How am I responsible for that? She was 28 years old. And right then, that painting my granddaughter had done fell off the wall and hit him on the head. True. It still gives me goosebumps today. I think God was saying: "Did you get that, mister?"

'There are grandparents out there who are raising 14 grandchildren. We have a lot who are raising five to eight. They come from every ethnic background. There are grandparents who have come here from other countries to raise the grandchildren, particularly from Australia. We have documentation for them — a handbook pack goes out, depending on the age of the children. We have worked with Family Planning on information for grandparents to use to teach sexual health to their grandchildren. This is necessary. We have baby packs. We have DVDs for grandparents, to help them deal with grandchildren who have suffered trauma and abuse. We have monthly newsletters where we share our thoughts and feelings.

'For a grandparent to turn around and start parenting again, it is a huge task. The kids are not your normal grandchildren. They don't do the "Yes, Nanny. No, Nanny" thing. They are angry kids. A lot of them have got special needs. These kids feel they have failed their parents and that's why they don't live with them. These children blame themselves. They come with attachment disorders, and other issues. The grandparents have to deal with it, even though they themselves may well have their own health concerns as they age — heart disease, diabetes, hearing problems, mobility problems.

'The grandparents do it because they are family. They have a natural love for their grandchildren. We have done two lots of research, in 2005 and again in 2009, where we talked to children and caregivers who have been raising kids for four years or more. Out of this we know that the main reason parents are unable to raise the children is neglect, abuse, substance abuse, and mental illness. Our research tells us that 97 per cent of our database come to us with one of these conditions. There can also be the death of a parent. Grandparents want to keep these kids in their family. They don't want a lost generation out there. Our research proves that children thrive better in whanau care. The tipuna leave a rich influence for these children. They know their history, their families. They are the best people to look after these children, but they need more support.

'More than 20,000 children are being raised informally in kinship care, not under the protection of CYF. Where a family isn't functioning, often a grandparent will step up and arrange to look after the kids. Some grandparents have to give up important jobs in order to raise their grandchildren; people who are nurses, lawyers, psychologists, doctors. They can take over informally with no orders over the children, or they do it formally, where they go to court and get orders over the children. This costs them a huge amount. We know that can be anything from $1500 to $200,000 in legal fees, depending on how contentious the court case is. You look at that amount of money being taken out of the older person's retirement funds. Then they have to turn around and raise the child until 18 years old, on a pittance.

'But they do it. Grandparents know the family. That is the children's identity. That is what cements their foundation base. That tells them:

this is where you belong, in this family. In my family, one of those little girls who was standing on the doormat listening to adults talking over her head slept that night, and for a long time afterwards, in the same room her mother had slept in. That's the continuity that creates identity.

'The grandparents might have been married for 40-plus years. The woman is normally the nurturing one, raising the grandchildren. The man might have worked all his life, and now he's finally free to play golf, travel the world or whatever, but all of a sudden he's back to a chaotic house, an over-tired wife. Some of these men leave the wife, and those children.

'The alternative for these children is foster care. We don't have the foster carers out there to take them in, even though foster carers get more financial support from government than kinship carers get. There are approximately 5000 children in foster care. In the latest statistics from Foster Care, some children have up to 11 foster placements a year.

'I see these elderly people at supervised access centres, where children have to go to see the parents who abused them. The children are clinging to the grandparents, saying, "Nanny, Nanny, please don't let go of me. Don't leave me." I look at the faces of the grandparents and feel their hurt.

'The tipuna leave a rich influence for these children.'

'Many of our grandparents tell us how much they love looking after their mokopuna. Grandparents don't expect raising children to be easy. They know that blood doesn't make a family. It is love in the heart that makes strong children. Children and old people belong together. Older people relish becoming a child again: we just want the time to look at bugs, leaves, watch a snail. We aren't rushing here and there like today's parents. We can sit down and look through old photo albums — talk about where we lived, the clothes, the pets, the holidays ... That is healthy for an older person's brain. It reboots their memories. But it's hard to do this 24/7, without a break, and with traumatised children. We do our best.

'And of course, those children often give that love back to us. That circle of love is what families are all about. Young Harry, the son of one of our foster daughters, is 21 and lives in our downstairs flat. He's an amazing young man. He makes sure we are okay. When he was growing up, they lived near. When he argued with his mum he used to get on his bike. She'd ring me and she'd say, "You've got incoming …", and sure enough he'd arrive on the doorstep. The spat was never anything that a warm hug, a hot meal and a bed for the night wouldn't cure. That's the importance of grandparents.

'And now? That boy downstairs looks after us. My husband's not well, and every night Harry comes upstairs after we've gone to bed and he cruises around, just making sure everything is fine. Then he goes back down. He never told us he did this and I never knew, until one night I wasn't asleep. I was in the kitchen having severe cluster headaches. My heart was pounding. I thought I was having a stroke. He came up when I was moaning and leaning over the kitchen bench with an ice flannel over my head. He said, "That's it, Nan. I'm taking you to hospital." He woke up Pop. He brought the car to the front. He held my hand all the way to hospital, stayed with me all night long, even though he had to go to work the next day. Love, that's what it's all about.'

♡

Vera Atiga-Anderson

'A big lounge is good'

'We are not a traditional Samoan family, but many Samoan families are like us. We have an ethnic and cultural mix amongst the family now. We adapt to whatever cultural practices are appropriate. I am a New Zealand-born Samoan German. My mum took me to Samoa when I was five. I learnt the language and culture there, and returned here for high school. I'm bilingual, bicultural. I trained as a stenographer,

and later trained as a teacher and a teacher-trainer. My husband is an Englishman. He was the key breadwinner, but I wanted to earn money, too, to make my contribution. When he was ill 10 years ago, I became the main breadwinner. Now I am the only breadwinner. I work full-time.

'We have one son and two daughters. My son was born in Samoa when I went back as an adult. The two girls were born here. I have raised all of my children here. Our children have had advantages and privileges in this beautiful country, a beautiful place to raise children. Now those advantages apply to my grandchildren, too.

'The language in our house is English. The children didn't learn Samoan while they were growing up, but they all are aware of their Samoan culture. My son, the eldest, married his childhood sweetheart, who is also Samoan. They have five children, but they live in Australia now, so I don't have hands-on access to those grandchildren. My son has been in Samoa more than his sisters have. He values his Samoan background highly. He promotes it in his home. He has a rule: if you are in the car with him, you speak Samoan, not English.

'It's different with my girls. They are very Kiwi. They speak mainly English, with just a little Samoan. They haven't married Samoans, so English is the common language for their families. I don't push my traditions onto them because we are such a mixture of cultures within the whole family. I'm always working out what works within each particular context. All of us are coming in from different backgrounds, including my sons-in-law.

'My older daughter is married to a European man who has some Cook Island blood. Their son, Caleb, is the only grandchild I have ready access to. He is four months old. I babysit him at least once a week. Because he is the only grandchild nearby, he is special to us. Caring for him is so much fun! It is one of the most enjoyable things in my life at the moment. I didn't have the time to enjoy it with my own children, but with grandparenting you have the luxury of not caring for them 24/7. I'm sure it is much more enjoyable being a grandmother than a mother. Maybe this is because the responsibility is shared.

'When Caleb was about to be born I asked my daughter if she wanted me there, and she said, "You can be on the periphery, but not right there when I'm giving birth." She wanted that to be just her and her husband, so I respected that. As soon as Caleb was born, I was the first to be rung. When they rang it was night-time. I packed up food and drink and flowers, and I drove like a mad woman through the traffic on the motorway. I was elated. I parked, ran up the stairs in the hospital, and that moment when I saw my daughter holding the baby, and me seeing her for the first time as a mum — that was quite something.

'Caleb just spreads joy throughout the whole family. Roy, my husband, is a man of very few words, but when Caleb was born Roy had this big, wide smile, and he was very happy. Every time Roy sees Caleb now, he just melts. We laugh at Roy, because we don't often see that side of him. Caleb also made his 89-year-old great-grandmother happy as well.

'I turned 60 at the same time that he was born, so there were milestones for both of us. People treated me differently. I was congratulated for being a grandmother. I think that's a Kiwi thing. It isn't a Samoan thing.

'At first he was a small baby, just seven pounds. Once he established breastfeeding he grew phenomenally, and when he filled out I could see the family traits. He's a gentle but stocky baby; he reminds me of a rugby player. I said to my daughter: "Do you think he is a forward?"

'He's like his mother, and seeing this brings back all those nurturing memories that I have of my own children at that age. I don't think you know what it is going to be like until you are a grandparent. It is so powerful. Whenever he does something new, I keep saying, "Julia, you were like this at your age." My daughter appreciates me more now. I have always been close to my children, but now Julia understands what I went through for them all — the sleepless nights, the worries, etc. — when they were babies.

'When I babysit for him, I talk a lot with him. I also sing to him. Because we are a Christian family, a lot of the music and stories are Christian ones. His mother would like to sing him Samoan songs, so she asks me questions about what songs to teach him, and basic vocabulary. That brings us all closer, too.

'Julia is a high-school teacher and graphic designer. She wants to look after him herself at home, so she doesn't need me to look after him while she goes to work, but I would quite happily look after him if she asked me. I know my mum did it for my sisters' children.

'Before Julia had the baby, she and her husband were big travellers. They have been in India, Nepal, Cambodia. At the moment it is very special having Julia here, so close, but I don't take it for granted. It doesn't matter where Caleb lives, so long as he is with his mum and dad and is loved and nurtured. If they want to go away, I will have to deal with that. I made up my mind a long time ago that I wouldn't encroach on their space or their decision-making. If they go away, I will miss the access to Caleb, but I will understand.

'Maybe I will take Caleb to visit Samoa when he is older. Who knows? I see the Australian grandchildren in Samoa when they are visiting there; I see them on Facebook.

'We all went to a family reunion in Samoa when my children were quite young. My kids were called palagi because they are fair-skinned. There were people there from New Zealand and Australia and Samoa. Our Samoan family members in Samoa live in towns, not in villages.

They live like most of us do here. They know their fa'a Samoa. They know how to behave in their island environment. The children all play outside, but they also now are all on screens and phones. My New Zealand-born members of the family know safety around water and the bush over there, and when they are here in the urban jungle, a different kind of jungle, they know how to behave here. I think of my children and their children as the post-modern citizens of the world.

'My duty is now as a matriarch who is the anchor for the extended family. I hear family stories that come down through oral history, through fagogo. I think I now have the role of handing those stories down. I do it with my girls now, and with other members of the family. Whenever there is a family event, they all come here to my home. I'm the oldest in my own family, so I am the mother hen. We don't have a big house, but the key thing is that the lounge is very big. A big lounge is key for Samoans and Maori. It's not the decoration that's important: the important thing is that we are all together. It's like the emotional space is key to my family, just being together.

'It is much more enjoyable being a grandmother than a mother.'

'A big lounge is good, but so is technology for keeping our family together. When Julia notices new behaviour in Caleb, or something odd with him, mainly to do with toileting at the moment, she will video it and put it on the internet for the whole family to enjoy and comment on. That way we keep up with one another. We all use Facebook and Facebook Messaging, and we Skype. Our family has its own website. Like I said, we have a post-modern approach to inter-generational contact.'

Back: Russell and Mac. Front: Jhan and Alyssa.

Russell Fransham and McGregor Smith

The importance of being connected

Mac told me he had been married to Wendy for 12 years and had two boys and two girls. 'When I met Russell and the marriage broke up, Wendy and I shared custody of our kids. Wendy has always been on-hand to be supportive. I was lucky she and I had respect for each other. I told the kids six months before I moved out just what was going to happen, so there were no surprises. It was like a countdown. And I only moved 30 minutes away. All they had to do was pick up the phone and I'd be there. I had one or another of the kids with me all the time. Hats off to Wendy. It wasn't an easy situation for her. It's turned out well; I now have two grandkids.'

The grandson, Jhan, and a mate of his, Grayson, were playing video games together while we were talking. Alyssa was playing with aunts and an uncle on the deck that juts out into a pond full of water lilies. We were in a hidden valley inland from Matapouri Bay, in Northland, in a magical environment full of rustling palms and bromeliads. Two dogs scampered through the house, then out onto a path that tunnelled away into deep undergrowth. 'One dog is ours. One is the grandkids'.'

Mac's partner, Russell, told me: 'Mac and I have been together 17 years. None of our grandchildren can remember anything other than this relationship of ours. I was married for four years and had one daughter. Initially, I didn't have custody when our marriage ended, but my daughter, Lena, came to live with me when she was 11 and stayed until her mid-teens. When she was 24, she had a daughter, Ebony, who is now 17. Lena moved to Australia to be closer to the baby's father, but that didn't work out. After four years they came back to Matapouri Bay, which has always been home. It's where Lena was born. They have recently moved to Wellington to give Ebony more opportunities.'

Mac: 'We've always been local, my siblings and I, almost next-door to each other, never too far away. When one sibling moved away from Dargaville to the coast, the others all moved, too. This helps with parenting and grandparenting. Jhan and Alyssa come over often. Erin, my daughter, their mum, is only across the island a short journey. Every long weekend they come here, to the valley. They always ask to come back. We are very close. Myself and Erin's friend and one of her brothers, we all helped cut Jhan's cord when he was born. Jhan and Erin spent his first three years here. I knew Erin was going to be a good mum. I'm from a big extended family, always been around kids. We are all nurturers. It was hard waking up at 2am for a feed, and then again for another one, and all those chores in the first year, but we all helped. And she did it. The contact is important. If the contact lags for any reason, it's time to do something about it, and we get over there or they come over here.'

I asked them what the grandkids do over here, in such an exquisite, mysterious garden, with towering trees, ponds full of perfumed lilies, ferns, palms and greenhouses; lots for a child to like, I thought.

Mac said: 'They like the bloody Wifi. That's what they like! It used to be other things, in the garden, but now they want to get on the computer, because where they live they don't have internet connection. The drawcard isn't helping Koro with the firewood or the pinecones or the chooks anymore. Now that Jhan is 11 and Alyssa seven, they are into the techno stuff. We let them go with it. Internet is vital for school. Just learning to be familiar with the machine is crucial. Their relationship with our place has changed. That doesn't matter. As long as they are here, and we are all part of each other's lives, and they want to be here, that's all that matters. My role as a grandfather has just evolved. This is the way every family is.'

Russell: 'When I first knew Mac, I went to meet him up in Whangarei and there were all these kids sitting around him, and he was playing the guitar and the kids were mesmerised. It was lovely to see. I always knew he liked kids. The kids have a lovely time with Mac, because he throws them around a lot. He tickles them and teases them. This morning Jhan was sulking about something, and Mac grabbed him and held him up above the lily pond and said, "Okay, snap out of it or you'll go lower" — little jerk towards the water — "lower". Another jerk, closer still. Jhan shrieked. I was with customers and it sounded as though Mac was cutting Zhan's throat, but it was just their teasing game.'

Mac said, 'It wasn't easy. He's heavy now. He's suddenly got long legs — he's all tall and gangly. It's like he's made out of a piece of string, but, man, there's some weight in those bones. I won't be able to do that much longer.'

We all thought a while, in silence, about the future. Mac said, 'My influence on both those two will be to just have a bloody big laugh, to not be too serious about anything. It's not my job. I'm confident Erin handles them well as a mother. My job is not responsibility. It's to be silly with the kids, to make fun with them. They need to learn to not treat life too seriously. I want them to be confident enough to take a few risks, to treat people well, to know where they come from.'

'I worry about our grandchildren's future,' said Russell. 'I worry about all the big stuff like climate change, social disruption, overpopulation. All of this is what is creating mayhem in the Middle East now, and along with that is the increasing divide between the haves and the have-nots. That's a gunpowder mix. It's going to end badly.'

So how does he prepare Ebony for that future?

'She hasn't shown interest in the plant stuff I do here, but I feel strongly that kids need to learn the basic life skills, growing food, living simply, doing without technology and electricity. We used to learn this as kids. I haven't really done it with Ebony. I used to go on about it 40 years ago. I was 15 when I found *Silent Spring* by Rachel Carson. I did a zoology degree and geography, and both of those disciplines were talking about climate change then. I also talked about overpopulation. I read Paul Ehrlich.'

Mac: 'I hope that the kids, just by watching what we are doing here with foods and stuff, will have this same concern about the future. It's important we can do for ourselves. I want the grandkids to be able to provide for themselves. Country people will be better able to survive than city people. We are both from farming families, raised on farms. We have lived in cities, but we never want to live in cities again.'

Russell: 'Our grandparents had to work out how to cope. They had a tough time just getting by, through the Depression and wars, and they taught us to be practical. It would be good to give that to our grandchildren. I lived in LA for a year, and a year in India. It was hugely instructive. I looked at India then, 1974, and I thought: "This is the future. We have to start to think that the whole world could be overcrowded like this."'

Mac nodded, then he went back to talking about teasing.

'Kids can drive you to desperation. You get to a point of explosion and the pressure gets too much. That's why laughter is so important. I tease them mercilessly. My father does exactly the same. He tormented all his kids. They loved it; at the same time they couldn't bear it. And they always came back for more. The grandkids have him as a great-grandfather, and he still pushes the tease buttons and knows how to get them giggling. Teasing is our family's way of relating. It's a great way of letting off steam and bonding at the same time.'

Russell: 'Ebony has been up here once since they went to Wellington.

It was a huge shock, from living in the country to living in Wellington. The first week she told me how cool and sophisticated the other girls were at school, but she phones less now. Your grandparents aren't your best friends when you are a teenager. But she's always very affectionate. I've been down a couple of times, and will go again soon. She's smart and creative. Her great-grandmother was an art teacher, and putting a high value on education and fostering a growing mind — these are important values in the family. I encouraged her in her creativity, and I encouraged her to make the move to a big city.'

The children came rushing through the lounge and out onto the deck. Jhan stopped, to tell me the important things about his koro. 'He gets me dog biscuits and chook scraps for presents. He gift-wraps them with bows on them. He's funny. He's not frightening. He threatens to throw me in the pond, but he's never done it. I know he wouldn't. There's some big eels in there.'

Mac added: 'They remember the trick presents more than the expensive presents they got at the same time. I might wrap up an onion for a present. The kids expect it. They'd be disappointed if they didn't get something like that.'

Alyssa chimed in: 'Koro is nice to me, too. He gives me chook scraps for Christmas.'

I asked about Christmases. 'Koro and Mum do the cooking. Russell maybe makes salads,' said Jhan.

'I'm not a great cook,' laughed Russell. He added that his lot are always here for Christmas Day. 'They adore these kids, too. They are aunties to them.'

Mac agrees about the cooking. 'There are always so many people here at Christmas, whanau, great-grandparents on both sides. This house is Family Central. Wendy comes to all these celebrations. That's her bed there, on the big window seat in the lounge. She often comes and stays a while. She cleans the kitchen. That's dreadful, I know, but it is what happens. We two are usually out in the dirt all day.'

The children ran off, past the piano, up the stairs.

'I don't sing much with the grandkids now, but I play piano for them and guitar sometimes,' said Mac. 'They aren't so interested in singing and playing now. You can present kids with an opportunity, and they choose which way to go, which natural inclination they have. If Jhan came to me and asked me to show him how to play the guitar, I'd show him. But one of his uncles, Adam, my second son, is an amazing guitarist. He'd show him. If they want to learn, there will be the support for it. First, they have to show me the direction they want to go in. I don't want carbon copies. I want them to be themselves.'

I asked about being gay grandparents.

Russell: 'Every family has gay members. The Homosexual Law Reform Bill's passing was a euphoric time. People had to stand up and be counted, but it didn't affect us. We've never had a problem about being gay. I wouldn't get married and neither would Mac. The worst way to tease Mac is to introduce him as my husband. He hates that. Attitudes didn't change because of the laws, but they change slowly, over generations, within families.'

Mac added that he thought civil unions were a crock of shit.

We decided I would take a family photo beside the pond, 'so I can just nudge them into the water,' said Mac. While I was taking the photo, Mac bent over his grandchildren and said, 'You are the stars.' The kids exploded away afterwards.

'I don't want carbon copies. I want them to be themselves.'

I asked them about their work.

'Mac has a bromeliad propagation business, and I have the tropical nursery, which I've been doing for 35 years. Mac developed the bromeliads in the early 1990s when living somewhere else. Now we overlap a lot with our work. There's always that anxiety of the self-employed: "My God, I should be out there doing something instead of sitting back." People come here to see the plants; carloads come through. There's the commercial side of the work, but we find that in our free time we also work at it, because it's a passion.'

Mac: 'I picked up some plants on a dumpsite, and that's when I started my interest in them. When I was teaching, I had the classroom like a forest. Some of the kids weren't interested in looking after them, but hopefully some of them left school appreciating it.'

Russell told me about the hibiscus 'Ebony River'. 'It has a very large bloom of coconut-ice pink edged with soft apricot, with a red eye. I sent Ebony the catalogue that mentions it. She took it to school. She's proud of it.'

Mac read from the catalogue: '*Neoregelia* "Alyssa". Long recurved leaves, flowering high in the centre. Forms a billowing rosette, and unusually (for *Neoregelia*), a stem.'

He pointed to an extraordinary bromeliad on the deck. 'That's *Dyckia* "Jhan".' I commented on its strange colour, almost black. 'An unusual metallic charcoal,' he quoted. 'Well stacked thick arched leaves. 1 metre tall flower spike of bright orange blooms. Heavily armed with large whitish spines.' Then he smiled and said, 'Not for the faint-hearted.' Like grandparenting, I guess.

♡

Sue and Wylie Evans

❧

'We can't possibly be strangers'

Wylie Evans has lived on his North Canterbury farm all of his life, but two of his three children live in England, and both he and wife, Sue, have grandchildren who were born there. Dougal lives in Hampshire with his English wife, Pip. They have Bella, three, and Lizzie, six months. Hannah lives in London with her English husband, Kris, and with Sidney, nine months old. When Sue and Wylie talked to me, Hannah and Sidney were on a plane, due to arrive in Christchurch soon and bring Sidney for his first trip to the farm. 'What I'm really looking forward to is taking him to the river. We have a dear little swimming hole down there, and for him just to be there …' said Wylie.

Sue and Wylie were in rural Warwickshire on a working holiday when Bella was born. Wylie was driving a combine harvester, and Sue cooked for the workers. The Evanses never go on holiday to loll around. Sue remembered: 'Dougal opened the door with this two-day-old baby in his arms! I thought she'd be tucked up in a bassinet. My memory of a baby is that they are in a bassinet or being carefully nursed, and here was our son jauntily carrying her around. He gave her to me; I was still standing in the entrance to their cottage, and I was stunned. You forget how small they are, how little. I was nervous. I felt better when I sat down and could get into a good position with her.'

Wylie explained how they keep in touch from the farm. 'We FaceTime them. Our internet connection isn't good at night, because so many people are using it now. But early in the morning it's brilliant. With Hannah in London, we wake up at six. She sits Sidney in his high-chair, and it's 5pm in London.'

Sue said, 'She puts the iPad on the table — and we are there! It's like having dinner with them, only we are sitting up in bed! We do this every day.'

'Not this morning,' said Wylie. 'This morning I knew she'd be heading for the airport to come to see us. Sue was outside, having breakfast on the deck. I thought I'd just try FaceTime, and, sure enough, she was in the car; Kris was driving along the M40 with Sidney asleep in the back in his rear-facing car-seat. Twenty years ago this was Sci Fi. Think of Maxwell Smart and the shoe-phone. We all thought that was crazy fantasy, but actually the only thing they got wrong was that they had a dial instead of push buttons.

'With the iPad being that much bigger than a phone, I reckon Sidney reacts to it. He grunts. He grins. When they arrive tomorrow, at Christchurch airport, it will be interesting to see if there is any recognition.'

Sue: 'I feel we can't possibly be strangers.

'At night she'll call us sometimes, and we see Sidney having his breakfast. Lunch is the only meal we've missed out on.'

Wylie: 'We try to FaceTime Dougal, Monday mornings our time. He's bathing Lizzie, and Pip does Bella, and he pops his phone in her crib and we see her trying to grab it. Bella says, "Hello." They sang "Happy Birthday" to their great-grandmother, Sue's mother, recently when she turned 100. Lizzie was seeking out Bella's hand while they were singing. It was lovely. The dog was there, too.

'These are the things that are really big for us. Getting pictures and messages. The two families all met up at the weekend and sent us photos of what they were doing together. It's instant gratification. You used to buy the film, take the photo, send it off to be developed, get the photos back a week later, then you'd have to post them.'

FaceTime can't be everything. Sue was a teacher, and she loves reading stories to children. 'Children's storybooks and their illustrations are wonderful. I love reading stories. I have read stories to Bella on FaceTime. I will be able to read stories to them both when they are older. I would have wanted to have Bella for a day a week and do things with her. I feel I'm missing out. I miss out on baking with them. When I was over there I didn't have a chance to do baking, because I didn't have my house. Just to be able to potter with them, to do the garden with them.

'When we've been over there, it's hard to get Bella and Lizzie on their own. When Pip went to work, her mother came to look after Bella! It felt like supervised access. But finally the other grandmother left, and we had Bella on our own for a while before Dougal came back from work. He was tickled pink that we were there with Bella by ourselves. Of course we do know it is wonderful that Pip is surrounded by her own lovely family there.

'We all went to Cornwall, to the beach, and Wylie made sandcastles on the beach with Bella. She said, "More water, Grandpa", and Wylie rushed off to get another bucket of water. She told her mother after that "Grandpa is my best friend." I didn't want to overcrowd her. I let Wylie do the hands-on. I was in the background wiping tables, keeping the show on the road.'

Sandcastles aren't the only things that Wylie is good at making. He spent 15 years building his own plane, which he then flew for 16 years.

Sue: 'When Sidney turned out to be a boy, Wylie said: "I'll build him a go-kart." '

Wylie: 'I had karts when I was a kid.'

Sue: 'And now Wylie chats to Sidney, and says, "Sidney, I need to discuss with you this go-kart." '

Wylie told me that the flight over for him now is an absolute grind. 'I get a sore back sitting in the plane. I hate it. I said one time, "No, that's enough." But I've actually been back twice since I said that!'

When Hannah wasn't coping with renovations, she called her capable parents and they went, straight away. Hannah and Kris's London flat had only one bedroom, so they were getting it extended to make room for baby Sidney. They were also getting a new bathroom and a new kitchen. They couldn't live there while the work was being done, not with a baby.

Sue: 'I bought a pair of overalls, Wylie packed his overalls and tools, and off we went. We cleaned and painted for six weeks — the whole place from top to bottom. We retiled some of the bathroom. The bathroom floor wasn't even. The builders had to redo it.'

Wylie: 'The shonkiest builders you could ever imagine.'

Sue: 'We camped in the London flat while we were doing it. It was winter. The kitchen where the French doors were to go had just a fence panel to close it off, with a big gap at the top. It was cold.'

Wylie: 'It was no holiday, I can tell you.'

Sue: 'We got quite chummy with the neighbours. It was a new experience for us being in a terraced house; not many of those in North Canterbury. There was no washbasin. I used to clean my teeth at the outside tap. I'd look along the yards, and people would wave, and there I was with my toothbrush. After we'd finished the bedroom, painted it, and oiled the floor, we got their bed out of storage and put it up, and we could actually sleep on a bed. We had our sleeping bags.'

'It'd be nice to have your grandchildren running to you.'

Wylie: 'We had to go over to Essex to pick up more tiles. Unfortunately the sat nav took us right through the middle of London. We incurred an £11 congestion charge. At one stage we could have reached out and touched St Paul's. Then the sat nav started going crazy because the buildings are too high and it couldn't get a proper reading. I knew we had to cross the river, and I could see it, so we went over Blackfriars

Bridge. We can laugh about it now, but it was a bit stressful at the time. A bit different from a muster!'

Sue: 'Ideally, we'd like our kids home, but the biggest thing is that they are happy where they are. We comfort ourselves with that. What if they were closer but in unhappy marriages? What would be the point of that?'

Wylie: 'We are lucky, our generation. We've had no war or Depression. We have work. Technology has gone ahead leaps and bounds. You didn't need higher education to get a job. Now we have problems looming with the climate, overpopulation, general unrest. I am a bit negative about the outlook for the future. I think this is a much safer part of the world to be in. It worries me slightly. There were riots in Clapham a few years ago. It doesn't take much to tip people over the edge. You can't keep people down all the time.'

Sue: 'You ignore the poor at your peril. Inequality is the biggest driver for any faction. It's dangerous. I want my grandchildren to be as adaptable and flexible as they can be, and with a give-it-a-go attitude that will make a difference. Things are not going to be as they have been. I hope for a good education for the grandchildren. They will then be able to cope with whatever comes.'

Wylie: 'It would be super if, when they were teenagers, the grandchildren came out here in like a gap year. We want to open bank accounts here for them so we can put money in at birthdays and Christmases for this. But it is ridiculously difficult here to open a bank account for someone overseas. We've tried. We have to get their birth certificates and do lots of paperwork.'

Sue: 'In 2013, we didn't go over, because that year I got two new hips. We don't think we'll go over next year, so we are missing a lot of Lizzie's early years. I haven't seen Lizzie. I've never held Lizzie. I haven't felt Lizzie. I feel I haven't quite welcomed her into the family.'

Wylie: 'I was playing bowls a year or two ago. A mate was there. His granddaughter came in and ran straight to him and hugged him. I said to him, "You're a lucky man, Jack." That's when you think it'd be nice to have your grandchildren running to you.'

Sue quickly made a joke of it: 'If we can't have our grandchildren living close to us, well, we'll just have two dogs.' And they do have.

From left: Fern, Mathew, Piripi, Anahera.

Piripi Whaanga

The koro shed

'I take my mokos on adventures. I like taking them into the bush. The mokos from Perth were over, and my brother and I, we took them into the bush, the Orongorongos. They've been in Oz for seven years. Tane was three then, and Maia was two. I tried to tell the parents not to come. They didn't get it. They both came! I took my own kids there, the five of them, years ago, along the track, taking off shoes and socks and wading across the river — oh, the excitement. It was dusk by the time we got to the hut. We felt it was a gigantic walk. They were fascinated by the hut.

It was because of that expedition that we repeated it with the mokos. I took food. We had backpacks to carry the kids in some of the time. I think Tane should have walked more than he did. And it was good that the parents came — it was a way of getting to know my son and his wife again, too.

'The kids were excited by the candles. We spent three days in there. We collected firewood. We built a big dam across the river. Abe, my son from Perth, was hovering around his kids. At times like that I wished it was just me and the mokos. My brother's into engineering, so the dam was amazing, and he set up a time-lapse camera to show us building the dam over the day. There were shots of us constructing it, and he even left it on overnight. He couldn't wait to get back to a computer to download it. "Hey," I thought, "who needs that as a record of being there?" I'd rather remember I was there because I knew I was there!

'I guess I cut across my sons' parenting styles. Tane threw food at me in the hut one day, so I put him outside. His dad disapproved of my action so much that he was speechless, but I think table manners are important. My other son and his wife, in Taranaki, are more relaxed about things, and they trust me totally with their kids; Arwen, the girl, and Shai, the boy, are in their teens or nearly. My son has made it easy for me to be with them, because he tells his kids, "Listen to Koro." They are respectful of me. A bit cheeky to their dad, but they think I'm relevant. They are pleased to see me. I've taken them away on trips, every two months, since they were born. We go swimming in the pool, and to river spots. Shai skates and has a scooter and goes surfing. Arwen is into collecting science-y things. This year we are hoping to get up on Taranaki, maybe stay in a hut overnight.

'On our car trips from Taranaki to Wellington, the adventure is the journey — the going up and down the hills. They don't need treats. Koro isn't the one who buys McDonald's. They've been brought up with the idea that between meals it is just fruit and water. If you are hungry, eat the fruit. If you are really lucky, you might get a sandwich. In the evenings I'm into books, and so is Arwen. They love board games. I hate board games, and they ace me in Monopoly or Caveman. They aren't into iPads and stuff.

Photo by Robbie Duncan

'The grandkids see your relationship with their parents, and they learn from that how to relate to you.'

'Two years ago, we went to Oz with son Kahu. "Eh son, I want to take the mokos to Oz to see the cousins." "Okay, Dad." Then Kahu says, "Can I come, too?" "Sure, son."

'We went for three weeks. It was fun. I took a ukulele. I've always had a guitar or a uke. We always have songs. I made up songs with their names in them. I wrote about 10 CDs of original songs. I record them on my laptop. I remember things by putting them into songs. There's one about Shai on the deck in the sun with Ohakea jets going over, when he was about two. For me, these are the best ways to bring back memories with the mokos.

'Speaking Maori is important to me. Kahu is the only one of my children who speaks Maori. He studied at polytech. This gave us another leg to our relationship. I'll talk in Maori on the phone to him. If we're tired, we often slip back into English. The point was always that we'd talk to the mokos in Maori and they'd be native speakers, but it hasn't happened. His partner doesn't speak Maori. If you don't have it spoken in the house, it won't work. Fern, my daughter Hana's three-year-old, has picked up lots of language from Playcentre. She'll point and say, "Manu, eh, bird?" But when the kids realise other people don't speak Maori, they tend to pull back.

'My father taught Maori to adults all his life, and he taught about what being Maori was. I learnt Maori chants and songs on the golf course from Dad. My mother was Irish. I'm Ngati Kahungungu and County Kerry. I think of myself as a cultural bridge, a kaitakawaenga. When you are a bridge you get lots of aches and pains, because people walk on you. I've spent a lot of my time between two cultural worlds. I'd like the moko not to be scared of Maori, and to pronounce it correctly. Now Shai is at secondary school, he might take it as a subject. He's doing haka, of course.

'I've given all my kids our whakapapa, which my dad worked on. It's a chart on the wall and it goes 30 generations down. The mokos are all on it. There's a brand-new moko from Hana, my daughter, so I'll have to add him to the charts. He's Mathew. And the big news is that Abe in Oz is coming home — and they have another moko on the way!

'Traditionally, there's giving the first-born up to the grandparents for them to look after. My children didn't do that. I would have liked the first-born grandson, to bring him up, but that's okay. I don't live through them. I have a full life. But they are part of who I am.

'Hana and her partner, Pete, and their kids live just a few streets away. I have to watch that I'm not round there too much, but when she's exhausted I turn up and help out. I take her kids to the Huia pool. Anahera just marches into the little kids' area until she swallows the water, then she spits it out. I don't show her my fear. I'm just there, close. I let them explore. In the bush I might say, "The fire is hot. Stay away", then I have to repeat "Hot. No", then it's "Yeah, that was hot, wasn't it?" They learn that way.

'Grandparents often think it is about them and the moko, but no; the grandkids see your relationship with their parents, and they learn from that how to relate to you. The moko are watching their parents, and they see their dad and mum trust the koro. You have to earn that trust by having a respectful relationship with your children first. I teach my moko the concept of mahinga — action. How you do things is the important thing, not the talking about it. You are what you do. I can die happy, with a smile on my face, if the mokos appreciate me and the family trust me.

'You can get offside with your parents when you are a teenager, and grandparents used to be the natural allies to go to. My Irish nana lived with us until she was 102. I understand what grandparents do, because of her example. She was widowed when she was 50, so she was always around. She was the backup to Mum.

'I have five children and one stepchild, and I've told all of them I won't store up money for them. I'll give them what money I have now. What they have to do with the money is build a koro shed. All five kids agreed. We are now looking at the koro flat in New Plymouth, and the one with Hana and Pete in Wellington. Josie in Carterton is planning one, too. When I'm much older I don't want to impose myself on the kids. I will trip around between them, from one self-contained koro shed to another. That's my retirement plan.'

Ro Crosby

❧

Looking after fragile things

The first thing I noticed in Ro's crowded sitting room was a collection of cake-decorating books. They were high up, on shelves, out of reach of small, searching hands. Some evenings, when she can fit it in, Ro ices cakes. Her work is exquisite, meticulous. 'I'm a cake decorator. I enjoy that. I normally make icing flowers, roses especially, for a shop in Feilding. She has great big boxes of them off me. I love to sit and make the roses.'

I asked her how she managed to post such delicate things so far, from the South Island.

'I wrap them in tissue, put Fragile tape all around the box. You have to look after fragile things.'

She showed me a box of her icing roses. Ro likes roses; I had noticed a well-cared-for rose bush in the battered front garden. She makes high-heel shoes out of icing — green ones, purple ones, white ones — for the wedding cakes. She concentrates and has a steady hand. She's known locally as 'The Cake Lady'.

'And I do some work for a lady in the Rangiora Cake Shop — flowers for her, little bits to put on cupcakes.'

Ro took down, from another equally high shelf, albums of photographs of the work that she's done. 'I have to keep them out of the way,' she said. 'I have standing orders from people. Like the other day a lady phoned and wanted three gluten-free cakes. Another lady wants four or five fruitcakes. She freezes them for her husband. I used to take orders from the hospitals. In a fortnight's time I have a wedding cake to be done, and another after Christmas. I do everything — the cake and the icing. When I was first married, I did a three-month course at night school. I didn't do any actual decorating until about 30 years ago, when I went to a six-week course and thoroughly enjoyed it. Then I did another class. Then I heard about a cake guild and asked if I could join. I did two years, learning, and then I joined it.'

As well as baking and decorating cakes, Ro knits intricate layettes for newborn babies. The one she was making right then was for her premature new great-grandson. She'll make others, too, for women in the prem baby unit who have seen the gorgeous clothes Ro's granddaughter is dressing her baby in.

To visit Ro, I had to phone from the deer-fence gates of the compound and wait. She came down the path through the garden, which is littered with exhausted toys, all lying on their sides, past that rose bush. She used a key to unlock the gate, and I quickly slipped through, then she padlocked it shut behind us. I noticed broken glass on the step when we went in the back door, through the kitchen and into the lounge, where the large TV was blaring at 9am.

Ro lives with James, her teenage grandson, and with Ben, her six-year-old great-grandson, born to her granddaughter, Emma, when Emma was in care, aged 16. Ben is autistic and ADHD. He is the reason for the padlock and the high fences.

'To be honest, he's quite hard work to look after,' she said. 'You just have to take everything as it comes. I must admit I do go to bed a bit earlier. Although, saying that, the busier I am, the more I seem to survive. Because I lost my husband six years ago, I was a bit on the lonely side. It was company, but I didn't realise it would wear me out.' Ro is 72.

'Emma's mum is Bernice, my youngest child. I have a son and two daughters, eight grandchildren, and five great-grandchildren so far. Emma has three now, and another granddaughter has two, a boy and a girl.

'The Welfare suggested my granddaughter — that's Emma — went to a place for young mums where they can be helped to budget, look after the baby, and all that. CYF promised to find her a home and set her up so she'd be able to cope. But none of that happened. Within three weeks they said she wasn't looking after the baby, which was ridiculous. She went out to see a friend and took the baby with her. They aren't allowed to take their babies out, so she was in trouble. She came back to stay with me, and went to school. I looked after Ben during the day and at night, while she slept. But one night I see her sitting texting away on two phones, and trying to feed him with a bottle under her chin. Well, I see red. I took him away from her. And I've had him ever since.

'The busier I am, the more I seem to survive.'

'When I took Ben on, he was the perfect baby. There never was anything wrong at all. He was very good all day, ate everything I gave him. He'd go to bed after his bath. I never had a problem with him waking up. I don't think he ever woke crying. No sicknesses. I was just so lucky, having this perfect baby. Then it all changed when he was about two and a half, and that's when he stopped eating. I found that hard. The only thing he would have was bottles and bottles of milk. He started all this bad behaviour. Just this year we've had him diagnosed as autistic and ADHD. He's got both.

'Ben likes to destroy everything. The bedroom is a right disaster. I don't have much wood on this side of the kitchen door where he's knocked and knocked and broken the wood away. He's broken the slats on his slat bed. I've bought new slats and put them on, and I've bought thin board to put over the top, thinking that would give a bit of extra support. He's broken that, and now I've bought some nails and I'm going to nail the wood on, hoping it will stay. So you never know what you will find in his room when you go in. He's broken sets of drawers. He's taken all the clothes out and scattered them all over the floor. He's got a big box of books: he can have them all over the floor, too. It keeps you on your toes constantly.

'Although he's been at school since February, we've only had an hour a day at first, then an hour and a half, and gradually a half-day. If there's a break, like school holidays, that throws him completely. So when he goes back, we really have to start again, getting him used to school. While he was at playschool, he was there three and a half days a week and he went all during the holidays. So he was in that good routine, which made things easier. I did have a break. But we've gone backwards because of the school system, but I'm hoping after Christmas, once he's settled again, give him a week or two, I hope they can then take him after lunch as well. That will be nice.

'I have lots of people who come to see Ben. About 12 people offer advice and see that he gets what he should have. Three or four of them are connected to the school. But there's no one-on-one teacher for him. He has a speech therapist. The class have accepted him now, but when he first went there he used to make horrible noises. You'd think he was a hurt little animal. That frightened the children. When Ben's put out, he screams, and that frightens them. In fine weather he's only in the class until about 11, and after that he can either play in the classroom or he can go outside in the sandpit or the jungle bars. But he's not learning enough. He might have to stay back with the beginners next year, and that will mean it's all new children in the classroom, but I guess he will have the same teacher. It's a worry that he can get out of the school grounds when no one is looking, and he can go across the road to the park. I think the education people are putting in a gate to try to stop him. There's a little fence all around, but that is no barrier for him at all.

'I normally have a little break when he's at school in the morning. I will sit on the computer then, with a cup of coffee. That's my break. Once he comes home I have to watch him all the time. If he can go to school for longer, that will give me the time, extra time, to do a few things I want to. I still have got lots I want to do. There are the cakes, of course, the decorating. I like to read, too, but that only happens when I go to bed in the winter months. I can get him to bed then, when it's dark. Other than that, it is just Ben. And I love the knitting, and I've just got two new great-grandchildren this year, born a week apart, one of each. The little girl in a prem unit, Ben's sister, she's coming on lovely now, and we are going to have her christened this week. My friends who are here from England right now are going to be her godparents. So that is something to look forward to. I like to garden, too, but that has to take a back seat when I'm quite busy with cakes. I really would love to take a floristry course as well. I'd like to make bouquets.'

I asked how Ro managed the cake decorating with Ben running around.

'When he gets a bit up, I get him a board out and some icing and some cutters, and he enjoys doing that. That keeps his attention. But some of it I do in the evenings if I've managed to get him to bed. Not often in the summer, though, because it's light, so that makes it difficult.

'He likes the TV all the time. While I'm in the room with him he's okay. So I sit and do my knitting. But around four o'clock he gets into screaming sessions. I put him in the bath. I have to keep watching him, because he turns the taps on, and normally the water can be right up to the top, overlapping onto the floor, if you leave him for a few seconds. Sometimes I walk out of the room for a few minutes. I know you shouldn't leave them on their own, but he's big enough.

'He doesn't like eating. Normally for breakfast I give him one slice of toast cut into four. He doesn't like butter, so it is completely blank. Nine out of 10 times the birds eat it. For lunch I give him a sandwich and two bits of fruit and a little bar that he likes, and this week I've bought Up & Go breakfasts. He likes those in his lunch instead of the sandwich. Come teatime it is red sausages with sauce. He likes yoghurts. He likes a McDonald's as a treat. But he throws the meat out, and just eats the bun. He likes Mountain Dew drinks. He found them in my bedroom. He eats no vegetables and no meat as such, except the sausages. Once in a while he'll have a boiled egg with soldiers. It makes you wonder how he survives on such limited food.'

'What's driving with Ben like?'

'I try to pick my times. In the mornings, like now, the pills are starting to take effect so he's okay. He'll go to school at this time, and he's fine in the car. I can take him shopping at this time in the morning, and it will be okay. Prior to him having medication, it was a nightmare to go shopping. I'd have to make all these promises, tell him what we are going to do. "Ben, when I stop the car we are going to get the trolley out — you get in the trolley. We go in the shop. Yes, yes." Then, when it comes to getting out of the car he might say, "I walk." I say, "No, Ben. I get the trolley." We'd have screams and fights. My daughter, Bernice, would mostly be holding him on the ground to try to calm him down. All the dirty looks we'd get! That was terrible. They'd be thinking: "Naughty child. Can't look after him." I felt like having a card with me that says "I'm not a naughty child." I might take him down to the supermarket now in the morning, when his pills are working, and have no problems. They are getting to know him there. At the deli counter they might ask him if he'd like to press the bell. He loves all that.

'The Ritalin pills don't last long enough. Some days we can get home from school okay. Yesterday we came home screaming. He brought something out of the school that he shouldn't have. And so we had all that on the way home. By three in the afternoon, the effect's gone completely. When I've asked if he can have more, they say he's on quite a high dose as it is.

'We have fights going to bed. If he feels it is his time to go to bed, that's fine, he'll just run in. But if he doesn't get into bed, that's when he can destroy everything. So I think someone is coming to see me this week. They want to put a camera in his room, and I will have an iPad to watch him. I can't really see what that is going to do, because I've tried to explain to them that I can watch him doing something on the screen and then go in there to stop him, but he's as quick as lightning, and he'll be out the door and I won't be able to get him back into bed. So, you can't win. Most of this week he's been up until 11 o'clock in his bedroom. We've had nights where he's got out of his room and

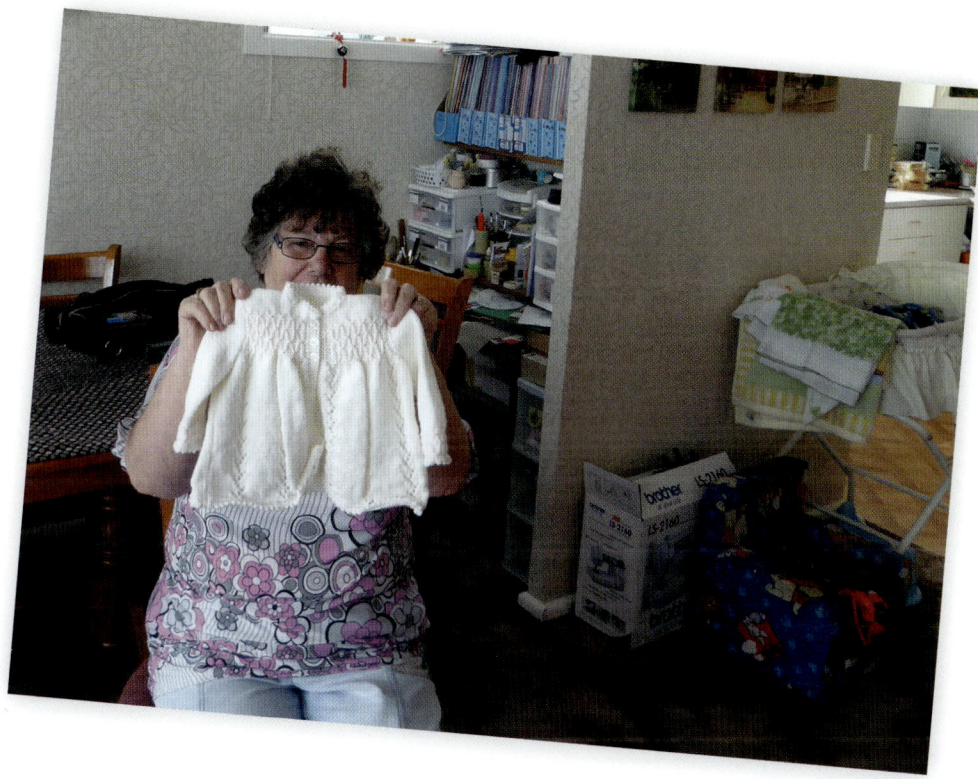

he's decided to go and watch TV. When he's screaming and carrying on there is no way you can pick him up. He's far too heavy and too strong. Sometimes we've had to sit up with him all night.'

James said that they had to do this one night recently, 'the night before my exam'.

Ro said, 'There have been times I've had to cancel school for both of them, because James has got to catch up on sleep. Ben hasn't been affected by it. He's stayed awake through until about 11am then gone to sleep for a little while. Then you have to hope that in the evening when it comes around to bath time, he's going to go to sleep. I've just bought some lavender to put in the bath to calm him down. I hope that works.'

'What is in the future for Ben?'

'I'd like to see him settle more so he can do schoolwork. He can write "Ben", but he can't read, or write anything else. I'd like to see him settle, to get an education. I'd like him to get the help he needs, so that, when he's a little older, he doesn't get knocked around by strangers. We've looked after him all this time, and I want people to be more aware of what is going on for him so they can help these children. It isn't until you have one of these children yourself that you realise just how many there are out there. Deep down he is a lovely little fella, and he never asked to be born like this.'

James, the brother of Ben's mother, Emma, told me he likes living with his grandmother. He's been here for three years and likes to help her. 'Ben's strong,' he said.

Ro said: 'He's a big help to me when Ben kicks off.'

James is ADHD as well, and had trouble at a previous school with other kids. 'Up here is quieter.'

While I was talking to Ro, James and Ben were outside collecting ladybirds and putting them in a jar.

Ro told me that Ben's mother, Emma, her granddaughter, now has two other children, a boy aged one, called Noah, and the new prem baby. 'I'm working with CYF at the moment so that, should anything happen to me, that is where Ben is to go, to his mother. They keep suggesting that his mother won't be able to cope and that he will have to go elsewhere, and that frightens me. These children don't like changes. So, because he's all right with his mum, and she now lives with my daughter, her mother, so she does have help, the two of them between them could look after him if they had to. Ben can be so boisterous, but with these two babies, his half-brother and -sister, he loves them and he's so gentle. As Noah has grown during the year, Ben can pick him up and give him a cuddle. He didn't want to know about the new baby when Emma told him she was going to have a little girl. But we took him up to the prem unit, and in he went, and he just stood there looking at her, and he was glued. We said, "Do you like your baby sister?", and he said, "She's lovely." And when we went back a week later Emma was able to pick her up, and she asked Ben if he'd like a cuddle, and he jumped up in that chair that quick, and he held her so gently and kept staring at her. It's really nice.

'Sometimes we've had to sit up with him all night.'

'I'm looking after all three of Emma's babies this afternoon and night, so Emma can go out tonight. She's going with sisters and friends. This is the first time since the new baby was born. She's got to start getting back into the world.'

When Ro showed me out, she pointed to the blooms on the rose bush in the front lawn.

'I often make up a bouquet and take it across to my husband in the cemetery. It's just across the road there.' She pointed through the deer fencing and over the busy road. 'If I had the time to do that floristry course I could make the bouquet that much nicer. You are never too old to learn.'

Marietjie Van Schalkwyk

❦

Making Skype interesting

'My daughter Marianne lives in London with her husband and their daughter, Jemima, who is five. They keep in touch using Skype. She was supposed to give birth two days after I arrived, but the morning of my flight we Skyped and she said, "Oh, I'm in pain." Her husband was walking up and down behind her on the screen, getting ready to go to work, and my husband and I both said, "Byron! You are not going to work today. You take Marianne to hospital right now." And he took her. We got on the plane. For a few hours I didn't have my phone on roaming, so I couldn't get hold of them. Jemima was born sooner than expected, and we arrived 24 hours late. When I got into that room it was just tears, tears all over.

'Byron is a very opinionated Kiwi bloke, and he had said to her, "We need to get everything organised, because we are getting two grandparents coming over from New Zealand and it's years since they had babies. So we have to put measures in place, because they will tell us what to do and that won't be good." So Marianne read a lot about breastfeeding and schedules. When she came home with the baby, she found out that book-learning isn't everything. She had this schedule which told her what to do every single hour! The first few nights Marianne and Byron were back and forth to the crying baby, and the schedule seemed to be breaking down. I heard all this commotion and I just thought, "Hmmm. I'm lying here reading *Pillars of the Earth* and I'm not going to help now. I'll leave them. I'll see how their schedule works out." I think at one in the morning I decided I would go in and see what was happening. I crept in, and Byron turned around and said, "High five! Your turn!", and the two new parents collapsed to sleep and left me with the baby. Marianne, after just two days, went all natural — demand feeding, co-sleeping, all natural. And that schedule went right out the window.

'We spent six weeks with them and our new grandchild. On the morning of our last day, when we had to say goodbye, I am on Marianne's bed. Marianne and the baby are there, and Jemima looked at me and smiled. I think it was a smile. And then there's this emptiness in me. You are leaving something that is very precious. Becoming a grandparent is like parenting: you have the same feelings. You get uncomfortable when the parents don't do what you think should be done. You have to be careful what you say. It's easier with a daughter than a son. You have a better relationship with a daughter and granddaughter than with a son. It's closer. So there was this emptiness.

'That's when I became adamant that we needed to do regular Skyping. I would not want Jemima to forget me. A big fear I had when we left her as a new baby was that we would have to re-introduce ourselves again the next time we saw her. That is the reason why I am trying to be as interactive as I can be on Skype. And she hasn't forgotten us. We Skype once a week to maintain a close relationship.

'When Jemima was little, Marianne was good at using Skype to get us to be part of her life. For her first birthday we were like a fly on the wall. No one knew we were there, but we could see everything that happened in the room. When Jemima had her first solids, Marianne sat her in front of the screen and said, 'Okay, she's going to have her first solids', and we were part of it.

'We Skyped weekly. I would have Marianne turn on Skype and I'd just watch her. They were coming over for a visit, and the day before they left I quickly Skyped them to say "I hope you have a good trip, safe travelling", but it was also the day of the final [2011] Rugby World Cup game, and Byron, that true Kiwi bloke, was sitting in his sitting room in London watching the game, and behind him is the desk with the computer where Marianne and Jemima are talking to me. Then Marianne says to me, "Could you look after Jemima for a while, because I have to iron some clothes before we pack?" So we are chatting, and playing away, Jemima and me, counting and singing. Then she started to try to climb off the chair and I thought: she's going to fall. I shouted,

"Byron, Byron! Quickly!" He jumped up and said, "Who Skypes when the Rugby World Cup final is on?" I said to him, "Byron, I am minding your child here." I am glad someone was watching!

'Sometimes in between the regular weekend Skypes, Marianne will Skype me and say, "I have to clean the house. Can you just look after Jemima while I vacuum?" So Jemima and I will do our thing, and then Marianne will come back and say, "Right, I'm done." So I'm still watching out for her.

'I read Hairy Maclary books to her, in English. She loves Hairy Maclary. My husband has a loud voice. When he reads to Jemima, his South African accent is strong and he sounds rough. She sometimes looks away from the book and says, "Sorry, Oupa, you can't read.' She calls him "Oupa" [Dutch and Afrikaans for "Grandad"]. I do a lot of reading to her on Skype. She needs to see the picture while I read. I realised when she was a bit older that I have to make this Skyping interesting, otherwise I'm not going to get her attention as much as I'd like. Other grandparents might hold the book to the screen and then read. I do it by dramatising the story. I came up with hand-puppets and toys. I have one from *The Lion King*. It's small, but if you put it up to the camera it becomes a huge face and this is what she sees. And then we play with this character.'

Marietjie showed me all of her hand-puppets. 'Some of these little hand-puppets were her mother's toys when she was little. I have a set of three little dinosaurs. When the Flintstones were popular, I put these up against the screen. She loved them very much, and we decided that when Ouma visits Jemima, they will have to come, too. My husband went over first, and he took them. Oupa could do the voice of a dinosaur, and she loved that. After an extended stay the dinosaurs were meant to come back here, but I never saw them again. They stayed with her. I have another little doll who stayed in the dollhouse for a while. Jemima and I do exercises with this one. The doll jumps and kicks her leg, and the funny thing is that I would see Jemima's little legs while she was doing the exercise.

'We try to be as interactive as we can be on Skype.'

'A couple of years ago I went over and we stayed in Paris for a few days, and her mother tried to give her little bits of French. I remember how we went into a tearooms and she ordered a macaron. Back home here, I got on Skype and she asked for her favourite toy of the moment: "Where's your giraffe?" All my Skyping toys are kept in a bag downstairs and the computer is upstairs. I said he was on holiday. Then, when I had got him, I made him a beret and told her, "Here he is. He's come back from holiday. He went to France."

'My daughters were brought up in South Africa and we spoke Afrikaans. When Jemima was a baby, I talked to her in Afrikaans. Now we all talk to the grandchildren in English. Marianne decided Afrikaans is a niche language, English is more widely spoken, and Jemima should learn to speak it from the beginning. But sometimes I get a video clip of Jemima singing a song in Afrikaans. She starts in English with, "Hello, Ouma and Oupa. I am going to sing you a song in Afrikaans." Once Jemima had an instrument and Oupa had a harmonica, and together they made music. An orchestra. If Oupa isn't there when we Skype, Marianne can take a photo of him and put all three of us on the screen.

'Jemina is now five. She tells me all about her day, but there is a new problem. She has a little brother now, Isaac, and he isn't interested in Skyping. He runs up and down taking no notice of us, and he's toned down the Skype thing between us. I can tell she is missing it. He doesn't allow her to have that fun time with me. He does want Skype time, but on his own terms. Isaac wants to talk about diggers with Oupa. My husband has a digger and Isaac has a digger, and they share diggers on Skype.

'Jemima and Isaac even give us cups of tea over the screen. And they kiss us goodnight on the screen. The hard thing is keeping up with them as they change, as they age. I am not quite sure where she is at now. I can't see all the things that she is doing every day. The parents have to tell us what to buy them for presents. Sometimes I'm scared. I want to interact, but I need some new inspiration. What will grasp her now? I need to do a bit of research.

'Jemima and Isaac have other grandparents, and they also Skype them. These children have the concept of a grandparent as being something interactive on screen.

'I don't know if they will come back to New Zealand. Byron's job at HSBC would be difficult to replicate here. Marianne loves London. She loves the museums. The children play in the museums. It is such a different lifestyle. We upgrade our cars. They upgrade their buggy!

'We have a dollhouse and a tree house my husband built for them for when they did come back, for a rare holiday. I made a garden called the Secret Garden. Before they arrived I glued things to the leaves, like Two Dollar Shop butterflies and things like that. It's because we so rarely see them that when they do come it is so special. I really make a fuss when she comes, because I don't want her to forget us when she goes back to London.

'Marianne and her two sisters here also Skype each other, and the babies are a part of that. Junet and her South African husband live 500 metres down the road from us here. They have a daughter called Sunet, and we see her often. My baby daughter, Melissa, is married to a Hungarian, and they live in Paraparaumu. She has two babies. So there are a lot of us, and we all post videos on WhatsApp. I have videos of them all on my phone I can play any time.' On her phone, Marietjie showed me a video of Isaac singing 'Happy Birthday' to himself when he turned two, and another of the two London grandchildren playing little violins, then bowing to Ouma and Oupa.

Marietjie closed her phone.

'You know, this is more pleasure than we got from our children. It was all about coping when we were mothers, but now it is the most precious thing that exists.'

♡

Keng Mow Chen

❧

Sage advice

Keng Mow Chen celebrated his eightieth birthday in 2015. He and his wife are now retired and spend a lot of time with their family — they have six grandchildren — and the rest of their time reading and travelling. They study Chinese history and geography, and the Chinese philosophers Confucius and Laozi, and they take trips on cruise liners and explore the world. They have been to Russia, the Mediterranean, South America and, most exciting for them, to see antiquities in China. 'We went to temples on the sides of hills. We've been to the Silk Road.

We have an understanding of how ancient China is. We watch the Mandarin-speaking channels 28, 29, 33.' They are enjoying leisure after a life of extremely hard work.

'My wife's sister was here in New Zealand before us. She and her husband lived in Singapore for a couple of years. He talked to me about New Zealand and he said, "Why don't you go there?" I said, "Why not?" My family have been migrants for generations. My grandfather went to Tasmania as a slave goldminer, but Australia was very harsh to live in. Only men could go there. They didn't allow women to go because they didn't want them to multiply. So my poor grandmother singlehandedly brought up my father and her two other sons in Singapore. When my father was grown-up, he went back to China and married and brought his wife (my mother) back to Singapore. I was born in Singapore, as were my two sisters.

'We decided to come to New Zealand when our youngest daughter, Weng Cyan, was five. My wife's sister was here to welcome us. I had been in England, where I trained in mechanical engineering, so I had had exposure to foreign ways of living. I had learnt English there. I got a job here in an engineering firm for one year, with accommodation, but I didn't make enough money to bring up three children. Sometimes in life luck plays an important part, and it did for us.

'One day my wife, Siu Chee Chan, was in a corner shop in Panmure. She got talking to the Chinese woman in the shop who worked there part-time. Her husband had just passed away. She had a takeaway shop upstairs. Every successful man has a capable woman behind him. I am lucky there. My wife took the job of a cook in the takeaway shop. After a while I decided we could run the takeaway business ourselves. We are adventurous. We worked hard. We bought the lease on a small shop in Otahuhu. We expanded the shop. We had a good business. We worked there until we retired.'

Their three children also worked in the shop. The middle child, Weng Wai, said, 'We children helped. My brother, Weng Key, was good at cooking the burgers and chips. I would do the dishes.'

Keng Mow Chen said, 'We wanted to expose the children to hard work. Economically, it isn't easy to earn a living. It is a lesson for them. They come to the shop, and they see their parents working hard. The children are clever. They reflect on what they see. They take pity on us. So they think: how to pay back the parent? By studying better. Intelligence is only part of it. They had good luck and good fortune. In Singapore the competition is harder. They do better here, so there is incentive here for them to push further.'

Weng Wai's parents encouraged all of their children to read, read anything at all: comics like *Buster* and *Casper* were favourites. Weng Wai said, 'In Singapore, Father took us to secondhand book stores to find Enid Blyton and other favourite books.'

All of the children graduated from medical school and became doctors.

'In Singapore, I worked in environmental health,' said Keng Mow. 'Maybe that was an influence. Why don't you try to push your children as hard as possible? That is what Chinese say.'

Weng Wai smiled. 'They said, "Why don't you apply for medical school?" So I did — and I got in!'

So the question I asked Keng Mow Chen was: 'Do your grandchildren have the same drive to do better? Can you motivate them to study and work hard?'

'My wife and myself have been mostly Chinese-educated. We decided that when our children married we would let them make their own decisions. "Let them be independent," I said. "Let them grow out of the house and go out on their own." And therefore the grandchildren's upbringing is up to the children, their parents, to do. It is not for us. But we do have a long-distance concern. Sometimes we just hint to the parents about what they should do. It is as Confucius says: "When you are not in power, when you retire, don't do whatever you used to do in those days before you retired. You have to retire gracefully." Therefore my power, my authority, is over. Our duty is finished. But our moral duty isn't finished. We are still concerned about the kids. Sometimes we might say, "Why can't the grandchildren come and see us?" Not only that: when we see the grandchildren, we know if they have been properly brought up or not. But we don't tell the grandchildren what to do.

'We have three granddaughters from one daughter, Weng Wai, and two boys and one girl from our son. In traditional Chinese practices, the children born of the daughter are regarded as outsiders, as is the daughter. They belong to the daughter's husband's family. But we have been abroad, and we have studied, and we say children are children. Grandchildren are grandchildren. It doesn't matter if they are from the daughter or the son. So we treat the six of them equally.'

It was important to Keng Mow Chen that his children married Chinese people. They did. He is lucky in this, too. Weng Wai says it was important to her that she had her parents' blessing when she chose a husband. And the luck goes further. Keng Mow Chen says, 'Weng Wai's father-in-law — he made us very welcome when we visited China. We stayed in his apartment. We are like old friends.'

Keng Mow Chen says, 'We don't have regular family gathering times. They have their lives. I have a life. The only regular thing is the occasion of a birthday. And we phone each other all the time.'

When the family get together, three generations of them, they speak English. When Weng Wai was growing up in Singapore, they spoke English at home even though they were fluent in Mandarin at school. 'When we came here, my parents tried hard to get us to keep up with Mandarin, but it was a losing battle. It's amazing how quickly you forget Chinese if you aren't speaking it constantly.' The granddaughters are keen to learn Mandarin. They can learn it here at school now.

'You don't need to teach them what to do. You just show them by example.'

The grandparents, Weng Wai and her three daughters, and her sister and niece are all going to Singapore in two months' time. Keng Mow Chen says Singapore is still regarded as home. 'I still have my sister's and brother's families and cousins there. When the grandchildren go to Singapore, they like it as a visitor likes it. When children go anywhere new, it is interesting for them. The oldest granddaughter didn't like the heat. She found it hard to understand people. But she is keen to go this time.

'We babysat the granddaughters when my daughter and her husband went away last week. If we look after them, Grandmother sleeps over with them at their house, and during the day we take them to our place to play and do things, and then they go back to their home to sleep overnight just because it's easier. They are very good grandchildren. Well-trained. It's easier now, but when they were little they used to have food allergies, and that meant there was a big chart for Grandmother about what food to give them. It is the parents who decide what they eat, what they do.

'What did I do with the three granddaughters when Weng Wai went away and we were looking after them? Ask my wife. They are girls. When I am with the granddaughters, my wife is always with me. The children love to eat what my wife cooks for them. She is a great cook. She is very careful with their food — they have no milk or egg because of allergies — and she listens when my daughter tells them what they can and can't eat. She was a trained nurse in Singapore and England.'

Weng Wai says, 'The children love to go round there. If they can eat the majority of the things on the table, they are very happy. When I first had the children, my mum and dad were a lot more hands-on. They had only just retired, and they hadn't realised there were a lot of other things they could be doing! They looked after my eldest daughter and my brother's children. Suddenly they realised there was this whole world of things they now do, and they started to branch out. I was happy for them, because I thought that is what they should be doing rather than looking after my children all the time. So now they travel a lot. But they are always there if I need them. I ring them and they can come to babysit most of the time. We all live in Auckland. My brother and sister and parents all live in Bucklands Beach, and we are in Glendowie, which is just 17 minutes on a good day.'

'Don't let the children know what is ahead for them. Children are very flexible.'

Keng Mow Chen reflects on his role. 'My duty is to make sure my children are happy and fulfilled and content. But for my grandchildren I have a little kindle of hope that they will have a decent life, decent work, a decent family. But I don't hope anything glamorous whatever. Let the children do the thinking and the hard work, otherwise their brains and thinking will become rusted. I wish the same things for the girls and the boys. We love girls. When a boy marries, so much depends on the daughter-in-law. My daughter-in-law is very good. If the son marries a critical one, you better run off. We are lucky; my daughters have a good sister-in-law who is like a sister.

'Chinese philosophy is low-profile. It's all about wait and see. With a big tree, the bigger you are, you catch the biggest wind. But some of the winds are dangerous. When you have a low tree, you don't catch anything. You might think the Chinese are shy. They are not. They are working things out in their heads.

'I have seen a lot of things in my life. We are more tolerant and relaxed about what the grandchildren do than we would be if we had come here straight from China. We are not worried, because we know we have capable children. We have sensitivity. We can smell if something is not right. But we do not involve ourselves too much. If you do, you will not be welcome the next time you go to the house.

'Don't let the children know what is ahead for them. Children are very flexible. Let them be exposed to hardship in the right way. Sometimes families overprotect. If that happens, the children can get lost when they leave home.

'Children are born innocent, like a white sheet of paper. Whatever you draw on them will influence them their whole life. The Chinese say when you bend it this way, it will go this way. If you colour it black, it will be black their whole life. Therefore the primary education is by environmental influence from you in the family. Forget about the religion. It doesn't matter. You don't need to teach them what to do. You just show them by example. That is what we do.'

♡

Kate Harcourt

❧

'They colonise my spare room'

'I am a very useful grandmother. I'm right here; I live downstairs. That's what makes me so useful. Miranda, my daughter, and Stuart and the three children live upstairs. It's a lovely whanau relationship we all have. Thomasin has to be picked up from a bus stop at 4.15 in the afternoons. Pete has to be picked up if he doesn't bike to school, or we drop him off or take him somewhere. I'm in perpetual motion. Luckily, I still have my driver's licence. We'd be stuffed if I didn't have it. I'm an essential chauffeur. That is my principal occupation.

'We do have rules about going to and fro, upstairs and downstairs. I never barge in. I always yell and ask if anyone is home. I now have one of the grandchildren, one at a time, living down here with me, flatting. Peter came first. He colonised my spare room. Now he's swapped with Thomasin. She's painted a wall of the spare room pink, revolting pink I think. Peter's gone back upstairs now. There are only three bedrooms upstairs, so it gives them space. To have their own space, one of them needed to come down. This means I can't have anyone to stay, but that doesn't worry me too much. It's quite fun, although their room is a tip. Thomasin is just as bad as Peter was.

'There are no house rules about having a grandchild downstairs with me. I just say: "When you have some washing, put it by the washing machine and I'll do it for you." They get themselves up and breakfasted. Peter went through a nasty phase of getting me up at the crack of dawn so I could drive him to school. I refuse to do that now. I went in my pyjamas. This happened two or three times. "I will collect you, but I am not going to take you. You will have to sort yourself out." That's a house rule. In the evening they eat upstairs. I often go up for dinner, when I'm asked. I make a good macaroni cheese or spag Bol, but only on special occasions.'

'How did you come to have this perfect grandparent arrangement and such a beautiful apartment?' I asked.

'I loved the garden in Brooklyn, but it was lonely after my husband Peter died. I worried about being burgled. Then I moved into a townhouse, but it had three storeys; too many stairs. My knees started troubling me, and the bedroom was on the third floor. Miranda and Stuart were living in Newtown, and someone had been nicking her clothes off the clothesline. It was their idea that we should look for a house together. Stuart said, "Don't ask me to look for houses. You two go and do it. I'm filming." So I found this one. My part was two garages, a scungy old washhouse and an office. Upstairs was how it still is. We bought it, and I worked out the alteration so that it suited me. I got windows put in to look at the view. One very big window.' The view over Wellington harbour is spectacular. 'And a new kitchen. Peter was a baby at this time. It was chaotic. Then Thomasin arrived.

'It's been a huge success for us all. I am a built-in babysitter. I'm never

lonely. I'm perfectly happy being on my own, but being lonely and being on your own are two separate things. I don't watch TV, except to see son Gordon on *Fair Go*. I read endlessly, do crosswords, play Solitaire, and I'm responsible for the garden. I grow all of the vegetables for the family. Moving the compost bins is the next big job. The rest of them never do a single thing in the garden. I'm out there growing beans, lettuces, spinach, kale. The grandchildren have loads of homework, and they are not in the least bit interested in the garden. We have had hens, and now we are getting more. That will be a job they will have to do.

'I've had an important role as a story-reader. I taught them all of the nursery rhymes. You need the grammar that comes with that. Thomasin, when she was small, would get out of bed and come down here and go back up with me in tow, because she wanted me to sing her songs. I haven't read to them lately, because they are all voracious readers now.

That's something I've fostered, but I'm not solely responsible for that. Their parents read lots, too.

'I take Thomasin for piano lessons every week, and pay for them. She has duets she has to play, so I've been practising the bottom part of the latest duet. I enjoy that. I'd like to be able to do something like that for the Auckland grandchildren, but all I can do is ring them up. I miss seeing them grow. The eldest of Gordon's in Auckland is the same age as the youngest here, and they are great mates. I foster those sorts of relationships.

'They are given so many opportunities. I go and support the Wellington ones doing whatever they do. Last night we went to a film showing of a film Davida was in. She was a lead player. She was absolutely splendid. She was in every scene: she was totally unselfconscious — she just went ahead and did it. We don't make a big thing of it, though. It's just another job.

'I stumped up for some of the cost of a school trip taking in the battlefields of Europe that Peter went on. It's left him very thoughtful. He had only one day after they returned from Gallipoli before he had to go to Singapore for an inter-college debate. They did well. Kim Hill interviewed him. We went a few nights ago to a final of the schools' debate in one of the parliamentary rooms. They didn't win, but they did well. Peter is named after my husband. He has the same curly hair, and the same talents. He's a great debater. He doesn't much care for acting. It's not the career for him. I look at him and think, "Oh, you are so like Peter to look at." So that is lovely for him to have his name.

'My great regret is that Peter didn't know any of his grandchildren, because they were all born after he died.

'Thomasin has had a six-month stint on *Shortland Street*. She was a girl called Pixie. She had cancer of the knee, and they put Thomasin through the hoops. She went up and down to Auckland, stayed with a friend. I think she got very stressed during that time. It was hard work. And then her character got pneumonia and they killed her off. Dreadful scenes at the end of her lying as a corpse. It was awful! Six months was quite enough. Her school was very supportive. She kept up with her schoolwork. We are very proud of her. I haven't watched *Shortland Street* since. I've had enough of it.

'I support them doing whatever they do.'

'My grandchildren are so valuable to me. Once, about four years ago, I had a fall. I hit my head on the back of the car, broke my eye socket, my nose and an arm. We were having this fence built, and at night I forgot the pile of wood was there and went straight into it. I knocked myself out, senseless. The three children leapt to the rescue, which I later thought was remarkable. Thomasin, 11, ran upstairs and rang the ambulance. Davida, just six, washed blood off me. Pete, 13, came in the ambulance to hospital with me. They knew what to do and they did it. I'm terribly grateful to them for that.

'I fell again, after a book club meeting, in a very steep street in Kilbirnie. I found myself on the ground. That's why I have this drooping eye. It's taken over a year; it's nearly better. I stripped the skin off my fingers and was covered in blood. A man picked me up, and I got back into the car. The show must go on. I had to drive to collect Pete from school. When I got there, he said, "What's happened?" There was blood everywhere by then. "We go straight to the hospital," he said. And we did!'

♡

Marion Thompson

~~~

Knowing how to answer a child's questions

Regan and Devendra ring the doorbell and Marion lets them in. 'Hi, Mum!' shouts Regan. 'Me and Devendra are going to do some cooking. We need two eggs. We scooted over here. Devendra's brought you some lemons from their tree.'

The two 11-year-old boys, best mates at school, tell me about their baking skills.

'We're making triple-chocolate muffins. Usually me and Mum do the cooking. Lamb roll you get from Nosh for $12. And beef rolls, and kebabs. Me and Devendra cook well together. I bake a lot with my aunt, Angela. Lots of stuff at school; our home learning is all about cooking and measurement. I read the instructions on the packet.'

'He goes to Nosh with Angela and Bruce,' laughs Marion, 'and he comes with me to Countdown and get all the specials. He lives in the rich world with his aunt, and the poor world with me.'

Although Regan calls her 'Mum', Marion is his grandmother. There are photographs in the hall and in Regan's bedroom of himself and his mother, photographs taken when Regan was a baby.

'I have been fully involved with Regan right from Day One,' says Marion.

Three years ago, she started relieving at the school Regan goes to. She trained as an early childhood teacher, then became a play specialist at Starship for two years, then an area manager for Auckland Kindergarten when they were going through huge changes. She lectured at Manukau Tech in Early Childhood Education. Marion is highly competent.

'My passion is the emotional wellbeing of children. I am always going to advocate for their wellbeing. If a child is crying, I will go and support them.'

Regan enjoys dancing, sings, plays drums, and draws a lot. He has a syndrome of ticks, which causes him to sometimes jump and flap about. 'Never see that at school. Just at home,' says Marion. 'The neurologist says we have to allow him to do it. Research suggests it is connected to the drug ropinirol, which Nicole, his mother, was on for Parkinson's. My work as a play specialist and early childcare worker has trained me to look after this child. I know what to do. I am very experienced at looking after children. I know how to answer children's questions.'

And what questions there have been …

'A five-year-old goes to school and tells his friends his mummy died in a house fire. Those kids go home and tell their parents, and then the next day they come back to school and one kid tells Regan he was lying. Several others said she was well now because she's with God and Jesus. We don't take the Christian line. We do say she died and has gone to Heaven. "Heaven" is a word we use, because it's a horrific fact to cope with; the fact that someone you love has died. He said, "If she's well now, why isn't she with me?" So that's something I have watched carefully over the years.

'It's his birthday on Tuesday. This week has been difficult for us both. He was sitting over here on the first day of the holidays, and he said he was feeling a little bit of grief and a little bit of regret. I asked, "What about?" "Grief that my mummy is dead, and regret that she won't be with me for my birthday, and that none of my outer family will be here to celebrate my birthday."

'When a child is little, everyone is there to celebrate their birthday. When they are older, it gets less and less. He's noticing that that outer family isn't as significant as it was in the past. So, last night he was crying. He said, "All my friends at school think they know all of me. They don't. They don't know the loneliness I feel when I can't have my mummy to celebrate my birthday with me." '

Marion's daughter, Nicole, was diagnosed with Parkinson's at 27 years old. Regan is one of the few babies born to women with Parkinson's. Nicole, a single mother, was living in Wellington. She rang CYFs to get support when he was six days old. Marion couldn't stay down in Wellington as she had her work in Auckland. Marion organised a nanny, but she was unsatisfactory. CYFs decided that the only way Nicole could keep Regan was to move back to Auckland and stay with Marion.

'We packed up. I was hell-bent on keeping them together as long as possible. My other daughter came down to help at the CYFs meeting. We came back to Auckland, and I set about making sure Regan had secure attachments to me, his aunt and to his mother. But then, six months later, Nicole moved, because she wanted to be independent. I got a job at a childcare centre in Mangere, and commuted from Stanmore Bay to Mangere. I used to collect Regan, take him to the childcare centre, and drop him off with Nicole at the end of the day.

'Parkinson's is degenerative. Her body kept going stiff. She had emotional issues. We tried to do everything to support her. She moved back to Wellington on 29 January 2007. That was her choice. There were several CYFs interventions that followed. She was admitted to hospital several times. I had to go and get Regan, and then go to the hospital. They couldn't do any curative treatment in hospital, just Valium. She became increasingly mentally ill.

'In June the following year, we went down for Nicole's birthday. Regan was two and a half years then. Nicole kept making decisions, then changing her mind. Angela got a call, saying Regan was coming up here. Nicole suggested that Angela and her partner, Bruce, could look after Regan, and they said they would have to do it legally. We consulted a lawyer and psychologist to arrange it, but then Nicole refused to sign the papers. She demanded Regan back, and we had to let him go.

'I moved to a job in a Matamata kindergarten. I'd have school holidays off, so I could be with Nicole and Regan. It seemed as though we had a good plan in place. Each visit I found Regan's behaviour had become more disturbing. He was climbing up the pantry to get food, like a monkey. That is how he got food to feed his mother. At three years old, he had become her caregiver. Then near Christmas, I got called by CYFs, who said Regan was in care. We drove straight to Wellington. Nicole gave permission for me to take Regan. How I remember when detectives knocked on the neighbours' door, and there was Regan. He said, "Hello, my Nanny. Where have you been hiding?" The detective nearly cried. Then Regan saw his aunt, Angela, and said, "Hello, my Angela. Where have you been hiding?" We picked him up, signed the legal papers, and drove all the way home to Auckland. Bruce was cutting the lawn when we arrived. "Hello, Bruce," said Regan. "Where have you been hiding?"

'I was hell-bent on keeping them together as long as possible.'

'Of course, all this trauma impacted hugely on Regan's developmental processes. He went away to Wellington as a child able to do many things; he came back as a child who had lost upper-body strength. He's 11 now, and struggles with learning. The neurologist and psychologist say all of this is connected to trauma.

'I had to go to court to get custody of Regan, which was so hard as Nicole was our daughter. But it had to be done. Nicole was in a halfway house then. She was admitted to the psych unit at Wellington hospital for a while. We went down to see her. She told us she was having a meeting on Monday to decide whether they would release her. She already knew that on the Monday she would be going home. Who in their right mind sends a psychotic woman home, just after she has parted from her child and her mother? When we said goodbye to her, she was lying on the floor, having a drama because she was saying goodbye to her child. He just got up with his teddy and walked to the door. I said to her, "See you later, sweetie", and I walked straight to the door without looking, scooped Regan up and left. The day after that, she died — she'd set fire to her house.

'It is harder now than it was then. It is the ongoing stuff. It was fine when Regan was three. It isn't so fine now he is 11. I find it difficult. I have only just gone back to work.

'It was Angela who suggested Regan and I move to Auckland to be closer to her and Bruce. I had to face my own mortality. Regan was under CYFs care, so I was really his foster parent. I had to answer to them about what I would do with him if I died or got seriously ill. I always had Angela and Bruce as a backup. My thinking was: "If I die, you can't take over Regan if you are only seeing him once a month. You have to have a closer relationship."

'So we moved closer to Angela. I got a job at the childcare centre in Remuera. I was telling children every day that their mummies would come and pick them up, and all that time Regan was hanging around my leg, hearing this. I knew I should have left that job, but I stayed until he started school. When he started school, one of the girls he went to the childcare centre with turned up, so he had a friend at school. They used to have a play-date thing, but because I worked they said, "Oh, you won't be able to come to that." I should have gone to that. I should have left that job. It would have helped. Hindsight is good.

'We were at childcare from 7.30 in the morning to 5.30 at night. I would come home and we'd have takeaways three to four nights a week, because that was all I could do. He had a late bedtime. He missed out on some things to do with writing. There has been a subsequent struggle with his reading and writing.

'When he started school, I started taking more care of myself. I reduced my hours to 9 to 2.30, to make more time for him. I didn't like the after-school care he was going to. I made sure I was the person who dropped him off and picked him up. Then I stopped work and went on an invalid's benefit. Both Regan and I suffer from post-traumatic stress disorder.

'There's a subtle transition happening now, for both of us. I'm the stoic one. Fortunately, I have good health. I do get exhausted, and Angela occasionally gives me a holiday, a weekend off. My daughter is nearly 40, and she and Bruce are more mature and have stepped up. The last time I had a break I went to Dunedin, to see friends. Facebook is very good for me, connecting me with friends overseas. I started playing Scrabble. I don't go out; I don't have any money to go out. Everything is carefully budgeted. For instance, I spend $20 a week for petrol. That's it. I have one treat. I might buy three bottles of wine a year, but I treat myself to Lewis Road Creamery milk in my coffee and tea! And I buy sparkling water.

'And Regan is showing entrepreneurial skills. He wanted to go to Hawke's Bay to my nephew's wedding. I said, "If you raise the money for the airfare you can come." So he did! He sold his artworks. Another time he raised money with an art display outside. People from the neighbourhood came around and bought stuff. Then he wanted an Xbox. "You have to raise the money yourself," I said. He's doing it. When it goes into his bank account, it is earmarked "Xbox". When he has the right amount of money, he'll get it.

'I told Regan recently that when he turns 18 I am going to get a round-the-world ticket and put a knapsack on my back and I'm taking off. And you know what? Regan says he's coming with me!'

♡

Pat McKenzie

❦

Nine grandchildren in the water

Thirty-seven years ago, on the night of Pat's fortieth birthday in Te Puke, she was feeling tender; she had recently separated from her husband. Two days before, she'd had a weekend away in Wellington, at an encounter group, where, she says, she had cried all the time. The tears were partly because her eldest son had recently told her that he and his girlfriend were expecting a baby. They were unmarried, and 18 years old. This son, after the separation, was living with his father. The younger son, Ross, aged 15, was living with her. On that night of her birthday, Ross was killed in a car accident.

'These two kids, Chris and Marina, had to get married,' said Pat, 'but no one felt like a wedding. We put it off, but you can't stop a baby. Marina was five and a half months by the time they got married. I had to buy a dress to wear. I couldn't let those two down. Of course I didn't really care what I was wearing then, but just that one step, buying the dress, helped me in my grieving. I couldn't retreat into myself. I started to think about the baby after that, and it was the baby, the longing for the baby, that kept me sane. It was wonderful to have something to look forward to.

'I missed the birth, because Chris was phoning me to tell me Marina was in labour and he was phoning the wrong number. I got there when Nicola was 15 minutes old. First, my heart went out to the couple. I thought, "This isn't going to be easy: 18½, with a baby." They had no idea what to expect. Chris was the first among his peers to have a baby. I said to Marina, "When she's 16, you'll have to give her to me: she's Aries born and Aries rising, and you two will fight." But this didn't happen.

'Then I focused on my grandchild, Nicola. The first thing I did was uncurl her hands. I stroked each little finger out. I bonded with her right then. She looked like our family. She looked like one of her uncles, like Scott. I felt she was mine.

'I didn't give them advice, because I'd learnt by then not to. When they were newly married, I once told Chris he should be drying the dishes, and he said, "Mother, this is my house, and don't tell me what to do!" That was a learning moment for me: my teenage son telling me he made his own decisions now. I thought, "Point taken."

'They lived out at the beach for a while. I knitted things, but when I found that the young ones don't know how to wash hand-knitted clothes I stopped knitting. Best not to put yourself through it.

'I often had sole charge. When Nic was nine months old, the parents went out one night. It was after 9.30 and I was asleep on my feet, but Nic wasn't going to sleep. I didn't have a cot, and she thought it was great fun to keep rolling off the mattress. So I phoned the other grandparents. I knew they were having dinner out, so I phoned the restaurant. I told them that when they'd finished dinner could they please come and collect their granddaughter and take her home with them, because they had a cot at their place.

'Nicola is 36 now, and she's the station cook on a cattle station south of Katherine in Northern Territory, Australia. She rings me for cooking advice. The other day she phoned and said she was cooking for 16. I said, "That's hardly more than a family. It's nothing. What are you worried about?" She knows I grew up on a farm and got married at 19. She knows I milked cows, and that I know how to do things. She said: "Puddings. I can't think of lots of different puddings." I just happened to have a book called *365 Puddings*, so I posted it off to her. Nicola rang for my birthday the other day. We had a huge talk; she tells me what she's cooking.'

Pat laughed. Her partner, Keith, now does most of the cooking. 'But I do make the curry and rice rolls — my mother made them, then my sister, and now I make them for the whole family. Everyone likes them. But never, ever buy fat-reduced pastry.

'After Nicola, there were more babies: Keri, then Ashley. They are all coming in January, because Keri is getting married. She has been with her partner for years, and they have three little boys, my great-grandchildren, aged 11, eight and five. I get on so well with them. I like little boys. I know what to do with them. They still like to snuggle and have stories, the eight-year-old particularly.'

Keri said, 'I loved the way Nana Pat had fairy pictures all over her toilet walls, and she dressed me up in long skirts like a fairy and took pictures of me in the garden. She loves to play cards with us, but doesn't love to lose. And she is really knowledgeable about our family tree, and is my go-to for questions about our Maori heritage.'

Pat said, 'I'm hoping to be the wise woman in the family, the woman with the stories.'

Nicola laughed and told me she could pour a brandy, lime and soda for Nana at age five (two fingers brandy, two fingers lime, then fill it up with soda). Desserts were always the much-loved icy slicey. And 'bloody kids' is one of Nana's favourite lines.

Pat continued: 'I love swimming in the sea at the Mount. I float around like a whale. Son Chris bought a house

> *'I'm hoping to be the wise woman in the family, the woman with the stories.'*

there for the whole family. I see Keri and the great-grandsons there. I don't take food, because she feeds them raw stuff. She's a health-food nut. I don't think they eat meat at all. If I'm going to the beach, the kids all come. Last Christmas, I had nine grandkids in the water. The eldest one was 11.

'I stand out there, past the second breaker, facing the shore, watching them all. We were down the beach getting pipis just after the tsunami happened in Samoa. One of the little ones shouted, "Nana, that's a big wave! Behind you!" I was terrified. It was a bad moment. Of course she meant a wave that came up to her knees!

'I don't swim when there are that many grandchildren and great-grandchildren to look after. I just count heads. A wave goes past, and then I count: 1, 2, 3, 4, 5, 6, 7, 8, 9. All there. Nine wet heads. Then another wave comes and I count again. I keep counting. I'm not losing any of them. No way. They are all mine.'

Isabella Tanielu-Dick

Emotional and financial support

'My grandchildren are from my eldest son, from two different ladies. My son was only 17 when his daughter, my first grandchild, was born. We were about to go out to dinner on my birthday. I got a call from my son saying, "Happy birthday, Mum. You got a granddaughter." That was a great joy to me. A granddaughter, and on my birthday! But she didn't get my name! They called her Aayliah.

'They started out living with us, and we were involved in the caring for the baby. Unfortunately, the relationship didn't last. I think it was my son who decided he didn't want to be stuck in this relationship. He left her for another woman. Because of this rift between my son and the mother of our grandchild, we didn't see Aayliah for what seemed like a long time. I grieved for her all that time, but I always remembered her birthdays and Christmas, providing gifts and things. She was three, then four. But then I found out that the mother of the woman's current partner is a workmate of mine! So I asked this person to see if she could explain my feelings, my grief, to the mother. If she could only explain how much I really wanted to see my grandchild. She said she would try. Close to the grandchild's fifth birthday, I got an invitation from the mother to come to Aayliah's birthday. Imagine that! I offered to make the cake. And I did. On the birthday morning I took the cake around, then we had another family event we had to attend. After that we went back to my granddaughter's party. My son didn't come. The mother still wouldn't see him. But that is the moment when my relationship with my granddaughter got back on track.

'The mother has married the partner now, and they have another child between them, a half-sister to my granddaughter. I try not to intrude into their family life, but all I want is to support my granddaughter in any way I can, in particular with her schooling. I said to Aayliah, "My home is also your home. I'm only across the bridge. You want anything, you let me know. You want to come for the weekend, you let me know. If we want you to come to family events, we will let you know. But all the other days you stay with Mum." So that is the arrangement that we have.

'The same son of mine started another relationship, with another local girl. Aayliah's mother is European/Maori. The new partner is European/Filipino. They have a daughter, Mia. From the age of nine months, that granddaughter and her parents lived with us until about three years ago. She is 10 now. Aayliah is 12.

'I love the girls. I can see differences between the two. The older one is reserved, quiet. The younger one is outgoing, confident. Part of the reason is that the little one was socialised right from the beginning in our childcare centre full-time until she was five. This allowed her to develop relationships with other children and teachers. Aayliah takes responsibility for her little half-sister. Mia is the only child in her family, and is surrounded by adults. Mia looks up to Aayliah.

'I see my role as teaching them their Samoan heritage. I do this by exposing them to cultural activities, taking them to family get-togethers. I was born and raised in Samoa. I came here when I was 15 to go to school, then I worked, and through that I met and married a palagi nurse. I encourage the girls to say their karakia or tatalo in Samoan, and especially their grace before food. Mia, the Filipino one, recites her grace beautifully. Aayliah says her grace in Maori. That's fine, because her mother is Maori. So long as you know you must thank God for the food you are about to eat, it doesn't matter what language you do it in. At home here, they are exposed to a lot of Samoan language. My whole family speaks Samoan. I used the Samoan language with my children. They attended Samoan-language Sunday school. Mia is particularly proud to tell people she is Samoan, Filipino and Pakeha. I think the bitterness between her mother and father makes Aayliah reluctant to acknowledge her Samoan identity. She doesn't talk about it much. She strongly identifies as Maori, because she identifies with her mother.

'When they go to church with me, I expect them to respect it and dress appropriately. No pants. They go in skirt or puletasi — that's a lavalava and top. My daughter knows not to wear tights — or if she does, to wear a lavalava on top of them when we have men around.

'Since my elder sister passed away, I am the one with the home that all the family comes to. When they come here, everything revolves around the Samoan culture. In the Samoan way of child-rearing, you direct children, tell them what to do. My ideas have changed a bit in this regard, because of my early childhood training. I think more now about serving, listening, guiding them.

'We read together. I even went and bought a little simplified version of the Bible so the grandchildren can understand it. I wrote their names on it. I told Mia the story of "Sina and the Tuna", and about the coconut tree, and ever since then coconuts have fascinated her. This story is often told at preschools in Samoa. We go to a market and Mia goes straight to the coconuts and starts looking for the eyes and a mouth, because they are the tuna from "Sina and the Tuna". She now wants to visit the pool in Samoa from the story. I have taken students there four times in the past to visit this mythical place. I'd like to take Mia and Aayliah to these places. Mia saw photos of my other son and his girlfriend, who went home to Samoa, and they were swimming with turtles in a pool, and Mia said, "Nana, I want to swim with turtles in a pool", and I said, "You will do all this when we go home for the reunion." A lot of Samoans have never been to these special places, because they haven't travelled around Samoa.

'I haven't taken my granddaughters home to Samoa yet. We are hoping to have a family reunion at the end of 2018, and I am planning to take them then. I did take them to Auckland in December to a big family gathering. My brothers and sisters and all our grandchildren were together. That was a great joy for me to have both my granddaughters attend our family meal and meet all their other cousins and second-cousins.

'I do play a big part supporting them emotionally and financially. Aayliah and Mia always say they love their nana. They'll tell you it's because I always take them shopping. When they come over here I look at their clothes and I notice if they are not washed properly or if they aren't wearing enough. I take them to buy clothes when the sales are on. It isn't about material things; I'm teaching them the value of things. One day I took them to The Warehouse. Aayliah went straight to a dress and said, "Nana, I want this dress." I looked at it, and it was $29.95, which is a lot of money for me. I don't buy things at that price. I wait until they go on sale. So I said, "Nana doesn't have enough money for that. How about we wait until the sale is on? You have to consider that there's always a time when prices go down." And then I forgot about the dress. My shopping rule is that if I feel it is crucial to their learning, I will buy it at its face value. If I feel it is something that they can wait for, they wait. But next time we went to The Warehouse, Aayliah made a beeline to the dress, and she couldn't believe it — it was $2.97! We checked with the checker, and it really was right. I said, "You can take that dress home." She was so excited. And then, next minute, I heard this funny thing. Mia was wanting this and that, and I heard Aayliah saying, "Mia,

'I am teaching them the value of money.'

look at it. It is too expensive. There must be cheaper ones!" So they are learning the value of money. I am teaching them this.

'Now my son is with another lady who brings two children from previous relationships. Mia is with these two step-siblings every alternate week, whereas Aayliah doesn't have much to do with those other two. Aayliah hasn't developed a relationship with her father. She doesn't want to call him "Father". She calls her step-father "Father", which I understand. I can also understand how my son is hurting because his eldest daughter doesn't call him "Dad". Aayliah said to me, "Don't force me to call him 'Dad'." I told her I wouldn't force her.

'I do my best to teach them to respect one another. I emphasise the importance of caring for one another, supporting each other and sharing. I always remind them to share what they have with others. My father is a minister of the church. He says it is all about serving people; it's never about creating wealth for ourselves. My husband, being palagi, took a long time to understand how I give away a lot of money or resources. I hope my granddaughters will continue this legacy.

'When school started this year, my Aayliah has gone to her new school, intermediate. I bought her uniform, and her stationery. She didn't phone me to tell me how her new school was going, so I rang her and I left a message: "Give me a call." She rang. "Nana, I have been busy. I haven't got my uniform yet. It will come next week." "How is school?" I asked. "It's okay."

'She's close to me and to her aunties. I had a mild heart attack last year, and she even said to my husband when he was driving her from the hospital, "Thank you, Grandad, for ringing the ambulance. Thank you very much." Steve was quite surprised. He said, "What do you think would happen if I didn't phone?" She said, "Well, I think Nana would be gone!" She cares.'

♡

Jenny and Tony Pritchard

Four grandparents, all together

Jenny and Tony live an hour's drive from their eldest grandson, Jamie, the son of their second son, Stephen. Tony told me: 'It's a relief to have grandchildren. Once we thought that was the end of the line for the family, but now it continues. When Jamie was born, his parents were in their mid-thirties. It was the same for his other two grandparents: they were also first-time grandparents. So it was very exciting for everybody. All us four grandparents were often together, sharing this precious grandchild. We all get on. We all feel the same love, and have the same goals for him.'

Jenny: 'We knew Jamie was different — we knew probably before his parents. I've taught autistic children at secondary school, and we started to notice little signs. We talked to each other about how to approach the parents, then we talked to them and they were also noticing these signs. We all knew we were coming to the same realisation, that something was different. Some stages in development weren't happening in Jamie; there was a lack of eye contact, hands continually flapping. He looked out the window at the trees, instead of at the people close by.

'With the other grandparents, we organised to have a Jamie Day once a fortnight, either at our place or at the other grandmother's. It was often all four grandparents and Jamie. It has become an important time for us and for him. The Jamie Day, as we call it, was to focus on his needs and to learn how to help him develop. He was in daycare — both his parents work full-time — and we felt he needed more one-to-one contact with people who loved him. We wanted to be part of his life, and for us, living a distance away, it was important to have a special time set aside for being with him.

'On the Jamie Day, throughout his preschool years, we took him to playgrounds, or swimming in the sea, ordinary activities. We weren't trying to put him on a special programme. We were just giving him the experience of play, laughter, interaction; things he got at home as well. He did have a person designated to look after him at daycare — a teacher aide — for some of the time, but we were able to give him so much more of that one-to-one. And being as there were three or often four of us, we could give each other a break during the day.

'We have had wonderful moments filled with laughter. One day we were here and I had cardboard rolls and ping-pong balls, and we put a ball into a roll and blew it and it popped out the other end. It was one of those precious moments when everyone was laughing together. And laughter is very important.

'You see a lot of changes in all children, of course, but it has been wonderful to see his progress. Two steps forward and one back at times, but that is progress. At first, when we used to take him out we had to be very careful where we took him. We had to avoid going anywhere where there were sudden noises or situations where he would get anxious. We can now take him to those places. When we first took him to the public library, he wouldn't go in because of the automatic gates that open and shut. But now he has no problem with them. In supermarkets, the bright lights and loud music do still disturb him. His parents don't take him to the supermarket. He and Ben, his younger brother, stay with his other grandmother, Jane, on Sunday mornings, and his parents do the weekly shop without distraction. He does still have meltdowns with us occasionally, and that is distressing.

'We don't get called "Grandad" and "Grandma". Jamie doesn't address us. He never has. He will say goodbye to each of us individually, but he doesn't ever say hello.

'Some autistic children don't like to be cuddled, but he does. When he is anxious, I'll ask him if he wants a cuddle, and that pressure of one person against the other, or your arms around him, that's part of the calming mechanism. If you don't do this, he could get too far-gone and have a meltdown.

'The Jamie Day still continues, even though he is now at school. We still pick him up from school at 3pm every Monday, and take him to his house and are with him until his mother gets home from work. When we pick him up from school, we might talk to his teacher aide briefly. Last year we picked him up on a Friday, and he had an individual learning plan. In it were the comments that the teacher and the aides had made during the week, so we could read that and see what had happened during his week. But all the dealing with the teachers and the decisions made about his education are the parents' decisions to make. We hope we are people they can discuss things with, but we are secondary. We are support.'

Both parents have challenging jobs. They also have Ben, who is full-on and active now, an inquisitive three-year-old. The four grandparents can offer the grandchildren different activities and interests. Jane, their other grandmother, lives close to them, so she's first call for babysitting and emergencies. The maternal grandfather can reinforce their Maori heritage. Tony enjoys indulging in physical play, and in using the computer as a teaching tool. Jenny, as an ex-teacher, has the patience.

Jenny: 'Jane and I both went on a course about learning to play. Three of us have been to a lecture about autism, and how to play with these children.'

Jamie is fascinated by light. When he was younger and could reach the light switch, he would turn the switches on and off, so Tony made him a light-box, which he can carry around and switch the lights on and off. Different combinations of switches turn on different lights. 'This diverted him for a while from constantly switching the house lights on and off. It's pretty simple,' said Tony.

Not everything is simple. Tony admitted, 'I tend to get frustrated that Jamie can't receive instruction, and doesn't know what I'm trying to show him or tell him. As often as not, the iPad will give a warning that he's doing the wrong thing, and Jamie finds that funny, so he'll do nothing but that wrong thing repeatedly, and the whole point of the game is lost. However, we have done a lot of work on the iPad that's been useful as well. We try to find what he can do and likes to do on it, and build on that. We can put shapes together on-screen. There's one program where you trace over the letter and get a reward if you do this correctly. We watched Jamie do it, and we were saying it was time to go now, but we had to wait until he had finished the whole activity. That was good.

'Jamie also has hand problems, difficulty with his fingers, hyper-mobility, so we look for apps that will help there. We got an app in which you pinch crabs, and they make a strange noise when you pinch one. He loved that. That helped with his finger movements. He doesn't like having his hair cut, so we used an app showing the whole process. You can put the child's face in the app on-screen, grow hair on top of it, and then cut it. We find these useful apps through contacts with autism groups. We go once a month to a support group, where there are other parents and grandparents. We talk about things we have found that have been successful. Sometimes they have ideas. Sometimes we have ideas. It's a sharing process.

Jenny: 'His parents have taken up the idea of a social story. You take photos and put them with text into a story involving Jamie. He likes that. Jane has also made books for him, with photos. We have videoed him and shown him himself doing activities. That's important for him, too. His mother has videos of him reading stories, and he likes watching those. He will be seriously looking at a picture storybook, and then Ben will come along and dive-bomb him. The interaction between the two is interesting. Jamie tends to copy Ben. Although two years younger, Ben is the leader.

'That contrast between the two boys will increasingly demand more imaginative behaviours from the two of us, because they both have such different needs. That's the benefit of there being two of us. Or four of us. I tend to do things with Jamie, and Tony tends to do things with Ben.

'With Jamie you have to find the moment. When the moment comes, you have to do the playing with him at his level. On Monday after he'd had his afternoon tea, I noticed the hula-hoop. I was showing him how to spin it, and then Jamie was doing it and inventing the game.'

Tony has a different way of seizing moments in Jamie's life and making something of them. 'Sometimes I have feelings about something, but it's not a story. It's just a feeling. And I like the challenge of shaping that feeling into a haiku.'

Tony has worked with an editor to publish and print three books of New Zealand haiku. 'This got me interested in the whole thing of little moments captured and put down on paper.

> Grandchildren giggle
> Together we share a grin
> I feel warm inside.

This haiku came out of a special moment when I had both boys laughing at the same thing I had shown them. We have a few YouTube clips of funny moments we have collected from various sources, and they demand to see them. They say, "Again. Again …" '

Jenny and Tony also have family days in their house beside the sea, up the coast from where Jamie lives. Jenny told me, 'Sometimes the other grandparents come out here on these days, too. We all realise that family is about just being there. Often the parents are tired at these gatherings, and that's fine. They can snooze while we just do what grandparents do. When they've all gone home, it is always an early night for us. At Christmas there was a moment when the whole family was together at Jane's place. The two boys were playing together with a crane, and that was quite a big breakthrough. None of us four had ever seen it in quite the same way before.

'Jamie has a strong sense of family. His Uncle Michael, our eldest son, was here last week, and Jamie had no hesitation about coming into the room because there was someone different there. Michael is spina bifida, and in a wheelchair, and could be intimidating to some kids. He comes down a few times a year, or, when the family drive up to Auckland, they will call in at Michael's. Our daughter, Alison, is in Australia. Jamie and Ben have a younger Australian cousin, Indie. When she was just five months old, they stayed here for a month. Whenever Jamie is here we often Skype Alison in Oz, and we

'We have the time. We can make sure the grandchildren see plenty of the sky.'

show the boys Indie's pictures. They both can say "Indie". I showed Jamie a photo on Monday, and he immediately said "Indie".'

Tony: 'Our theory is that the children will want to put the iPad down and go outside if they know what outside is like, so we show them plenty of outside. Even with Michael and walking with crutches, we took him tramping. It gave him an experience, and he was able to appreciate the outdoors. We have the time. We can make sure the grandchildren see plenty of the sky.

'Jamie loves the sea. The feeling of the water is important to him, and watching the water move. It's a sensory thing. I think the water itself supports his body. He always enjoys being in the sea. It's a calm, shallow beach here, so it is safe. It doesn't matter to him if the water is cold — but it does to us! If he wades out too far, we shout at each other: "Go and get him." "Look, it's only up to his chest." "I know, but go and get him!" "'You!" "No! You!" There is always a worry about the sea. You can't call his name and get a response.

'In the future, we hope for a happy, independent life for him, the same as anyone wants for a grandchild. Being able to live independently, that's what we are hoping for.'

Jenny said, 'We are going to have a Ben Day, just as we had a Jamie Day, where we will be taking Ben out of daycare for a regular day.'

Tony added, 'We will all have to be fit to keep up with him!'

I had met the whirlwind that is Ben. I left with an image of four grandparents running along the beach after one small boy, a boy who will ignore their shouts of "Ben! Stop!", but for quite different reasons from Jamie's.

Grandparents need to learn how to use

- A baby monitor.
- Baby sleeping bags.
- A pushchair. Practise in the evening folding and unfolding it. It is a good exercise to keep the brain young and challenged.
- An iPad and smart-phone apps.
- Instructions that come with gifts that require construction.
- The word 'organic'.
- A car booster seat. Practise strapping it into the car before you pick up the child.
- Child-proof bottles. Toilet-bowl cleaner and bleach are now stored out of reach. We have to get the grandkids to get them down *and* undo them for us.

Judith and Colin Cowie

❦

Spending a lot of time on the sidelines

Colin appoints the referees for the North Harbour Rugby Union Saturday mornings' sport, and for the junior boys. He is there, at the games, every Saturday morning, watching the games, particularly watching the referees starting out. He coaches them. 'I've been involved actively or administratively for about 40 years now. I have spent a lot of time walking up and down on the sidelines. I've always loved sport, particularly children's sport.'

Colin's coaching and encouraging of his own grandchildren started before they were even born. 'When the first grandchild was due, I was teaching at Kaitaia Primary. One Friday afternoon, when the birth was imminent, we were at a school assembly out on the asphalt, straight after lunch. The school didn't have a hall at that stage. I'd been down on the lower field, and it was quite wet. I had my gumboots on. We'd been doing a bit of line-dancing, and the kids thought that was hilarious, me dancing in my gumboots. I was doing my thing out in front with all the school, when the school secretary came running out and said the birth was happening and they needed me at the hospital. As soon as I heard that, I just said, "I'm away. This grandchild of ours is going to be born!" And off I went, gumboots and all, to do the most important coaching I'd done in my life up until then. And Shona, our daughter, maintains that if it hadn't been for me telling her to push, Hayden probably would never have come out!

'So naturally Hayden's had a fair bit of coaching input. At secondary school, he wanted to play cricket on Saturday mornings. Wayne, his dad, works in retail, so he was always busy Saturdays. I took Hayden to practices, and I took it on myself to become Hayden's cricket mentor. I did some coaching then to help out the team coach, but it was mainly as an umpire for the actual games that I took part. So that went from the time Hayden was 9 or 10 through to when he finished playing for the First XI at Birkenhead College.

'Sasha, his sister, played soccer for the same school. I didn't coach her team, but I was the regular support person. I took her and her mates to the games, and helped out on the sidelines when I could, but I also gave her coaching tips as part of her learning to play the game. Sasha always has a go at Shona, her mum, saying, "I don't think you've ever seen me play soccer, Mum. It was always Pop. He was always there."

'We probably had most to do with the youngest, Leah, because she was a baby when we first came down to Auckland. We took her to after-school activities, all of them — dance, learning to swim, stuff like that. And still now, Leah's 15, I'll take her to summer netball or touch rugby. I don't coach the team, but we'll discuss the game afterwards. We discuss her play, what she should do in order to better her performance.'

Colin has played most team sports. At secondary school, he played

'I encourage and suggest, rather than say "You did wrong."'

rugby and cricket. At teachers' college, he learnt to coach netball and hockey. Doing his OE in Vancouver, he learnt soccer, softball and volleyball coaching. In Australia, he played rugby on Saturday mornings, but coached rugby league in high schools. Back in New Zealand, he coached softball and rugby league, and started his long involvement as a rugby referee.

'For my eight grandchildren, I hope I've created a love of sport, and the quality in life that sport can give you: being a member of a team, contributing to others in their endeavours. Sometimes it can get frustrating when I know they don't take the opportunities that I see, but I've never been one of those adults who is hard on children. I encourage and suggest, rather than say "You did wrong." I know they do their best.

'If I'm there supporting the children, I don't ever shout at the ref.

With my background as a ref I'm always standing up for the referees.

'I've been fortunate to keep good health, and right until I finished active refereeing I kept myself mentally and physically fit in order to referee, and in the summer when umpiring senior cricket. You do have to be mentally and physically fit to continue with that. It is as exhausting standing out on the hot cricket pitch from 11am to 6pm as it is refereeing a rugby game between 2.30pm and 4pm.

'The grandchildren all respect my advice, because I have been the one who's been there for them, taken them to the game, supported them in their games and talked to them about sport. I always hoped one of the grandchildren would do something special with sport. There's always that Kiwi thing. When I was a kid I used to run around the farm imagining I was an All Black. My son Dean's second-to-eldest, Isabel, is a very good swimmer. She could make it. She's close to state times for swimming in Melbourne, where they live. She's also a good netballer.

'It's more difficult these days for children to commit to sport. They have studies, and Saturday jobs. Their sport gets put into the background. We didn't have that dilemma when I was young. Rugby wasn't over the length of time it is now. It started in early May, and you'd go through to August. We dried the cows off on Anzac Day, so in May we had only a morning milking of the house cow until they started coming in again in late July or August. My brother and I did most of the milking. My dad lost his right hand in the Home Guard during the war. He was doing exercises at Ninety Mile Beach and a grenade blew off his hand. He was the local school-bus driver. That had to go by the board. So, you learn to get by.

'I've heard people say you can't get anything out of teenagers until 10 o'clock in the morning. Look, it's a lot of rubbish. We used to milk cows, then run up the hill, have breakfast, run up to catch the bus and go to school. We had a deputy principal come up to Kaitaia from Whangarei Boys' High the year we were sitting School Certificate. He was giving us tips about sitting the French exam, and he told us that on the morning of the exam we should "have a browse through the textbook, have a leisurely breakfast and then come to school". One of us said, "What are we supposed to do with the book? Put it on the cow's back?" He hadn't realised that most of us were from farms. Many are the pieces of paper I've had on a cow's back. They've been splattered with cow muck because we did our study while we were milking! All those hours I've spent milking cows! I wasn't ever tempted to become a farmer. So, these teenagers, if they want to get up to do their thing, they will get up.

'I still take Leah and her friends to their sport. They play netball regardless of the weather. We've been at that court in Northcote, in the winter. You have an umbrella you can hardly hold because the wind is so strong there, and the rain is belting into your face. You try to look at the game from half-closed eyes while you are sheltering, and those girls are playing away there, in such skimpy clothes. It's tougher than what's expected of boys.

'Now Leah's thinking of taking up squash. I haven't been involved with squash yet, but I have played it. We had a holiday out of Melbourne once, to see the Australian grandchildren. There was a squash court there, and Hugh and his father, Dean, and I played together one morning, to show him how to play. Golf? I've never joined a club, but we used to get up early on Sunday morning and go to Chamberlain Park and play a round of golf with my sons.

'I could not have given all that time to coaching if it wasn't for Judith, my wife. She's been as much a supporter of the grandchildren as I have. She doesn't go to touch rugby on a Tuesday with the rest of us, because that is the night the whole family comes to dinner and she's busy cooking for them. That's our family time. All the grandchildren are encouraged to take part in conversation at the dinner table. It doesn't have to be about sport. Grandparents can help by respecting what the children say.

'We have time because we are retired, so we make time for the grandchildren. Shona will say, "If I want to know something I will ask Leah, because she'll have talked about it with Poppa and Nana." Judy and I are very proud of our grandchildren. We like spending time with them. We've always been available to help out, take them on holiday, even when they were little ones. Now they are grown-up, they are happy to spend some time with us.'

♡

Joan Hall

The importance of touch

'Fifty-three years ago I was a young woman travelling on a train from Dunedin to Christchurch. I'd had a fun week with a younger brother who was studying at Otago. The train stopped at Oamaru. I was just gazing out the window, thinking about all the parties I'd been to and the men I had met, when my attention was caught by this man, a father, kissing his red-headed son goodbye. Such a loving display of affection from a father struck me as unusual. There was an empty seat beside me, and the red-headed son sat down beside me. Five months later, we decided to marry. Fifty-three years later, I am still married to Ivan.

'When our three sons were growing up, Ivan was the most affectionate father I've seen. Ivan's father used to make breakfast all the time for his family; he was unusual for his time. Ivan had that same warmth about him that his father had. He kissed the boys always, and still does. And I have watched my big sons kissing their sons goodnight. I think, when I see that, "Ivan did well." Yes. It gives me such pleasure to see the way my boys are bringing up their sons, and I see so much of Ivan in that.

'Fergus, our eldest grandson, was born in Japan. His parents brought him back to New Zealand when he was just three weeks old, to meet the family. He was given to me when they came off the plane, and someone walked past me and said, "Hmm, born on the plane, was he?"

'They came back here every three months regularly for two years, then they returned to New Zealand permanently when Jackie was pregnant again, with Lachy. David, our eldest son, brought takeaways around to the Mount, where the family was all gathered to welcome them home. He was always late for everything, but not this day. He arrived at six, as promised. It seemed as though everything would be perfect after that, but three days later David died in a light-plane accident. He was 39, and had no children.

'Ivan and I eventually sold David's business, and then one day, just a few months after that, Ivan said he was worried he couldn't keep his grandsons' names sorted. So he went to the GP and was diagnosed with Alzheimer's and vascular dementia.

'Simon, the elder of our two remaining sons, now lives in Lower Hutt with Hilary and their two children. Justin and Jackie now live in Nelson with Fergus and Lachy. So suddenly the family was scattered — not out of touch, but out of touching range. When I visit either family, I'm always just a little bit anxious that it will be a good experience, for them as well as me.

'When David went off to Massey University, I can remember a phone conversation with him in which he said, "Mum, the thing I really miss is the physical contact we have at home. That's gone out of my life now." We always used to touch each other, and hug and kiss a lot. I miss the touching now. But I look at my sons and I see the warmth in the way they deal with their sons, and I think, "You'll do."

'It became difficult to take Ivan to visit the grandchildren or have family visit him here. I would put Ivan into respite care so that I could continue to visit the grandchildren, but when Ivan started climbing out of that place we had to find somewhere more permanent for him, somewhere close to me so I can visit frequently.

'I haven't seen as much of the children as many grandparents do. And whether things would have been different if Ivan hadn't become ill, I don't know. But I don't think I'm a hands-on grandparent. I don't want to be fully involved day-to-day. I'm willing to step in and help, but I have developed a life that I can live, that keeps me independent, and that's partly because I don't have the relationship with family that would fill some of the gaps. There are times now when the family have to organise their contacts with me around the things that I do, rather than assuming I am just here. I've never been a baby person, and I'm always uncertain as to how to deal with other people's babies.

'I'm not a good phone person, so I don't often keep in contact with the grandchildren by phone. It's partly because it's easier to talk to people if you are doing something with them. It's hard when you don't see them often. Sons are not as good at communicating family news as daughters are, and I have no daughters. From the sons the emails are always for a purpose. My daughters-in-law are good at keeping me in touch with what's going on, but I can't get to the events. I've missed the day-to-day things kids do, and increasingly I find there are fewer of the school break-ups and milestones that I attend. With Ivan ill, I haven't been free to go to them.

'It gives me such pleasure to see the way my boys are bringing up their sons.'

'The boys don't phone me. Sometimes I finish a conversation with their parents by talking to them, but the intensity of the conversation depends on my knowing what they've just been up to, and as I don't know their latest activities I can't say something about them. It's the not knowing the details of what is going on that makes it hard. It's a brief conversation as a general rule. It is harder for me to relate to the younger sons in each of the families also, because there's an elder brother blocking the way, between them and me.

'I miss the little things that build up the life of a relationship, but I get the spectacular news when it happens. Toby, in Lower Hutt, assembled a computer when he was 10. There was a huge bang — the thing exploded because he had connected the wrong things. He went to his parent–teacher interviews having prepared a PowerPoint presentation giving his point of view. That sort of thing delights me, but they don't rush home to tell me about it.

'But there have been visits to me. Simon suggested that his sons should come up, each boy on his own, to spend two days and a night with me. I had two delightful visits with these children. I did things I wouldn't have done. I went to a movie with one of them. I took the younger one, Jasper, to the Art Gallery, where there was a jewellery exhibition by New Zealand artists. A woman showed us about 30 blowflies painted all different colours and set up in an exhibit. And he saw a necklace that looked like little black beads painted with gold things in between, and these were rabbit poo. Jaspar was fascinated. It put us on a level of enjoyment that we hadn't really shared before.

'I've seen Fergus and Lachy — now teenagers — when they went off on a family holiday. I walked with Fergus in the airport, and he talked to me, non-stop, about how he was learning Japanese. I think I enjoy the children more as they grow older. I can have conversations with them now that they are more interested in adult things as well.

'The Lower Hutt family is moving to Sydney in January. I looked after the boys when Hilary went over to Sydney to find somewhere to rent. That time was so good. I knew in principle what they did, but seeing them doing it, being part of it and taking them to the library or Jaspar going off in his white uniform to Tae Kwon Do — I didn't even know he did that.

'Sons are not as good at communicating family news as daughters are.'

'While Ivan is still alive I won't visit them in Australia for long visits. Just short ones. I expect to be very warmly welcomed when I do see them. I don't know when they will come back.

'This grandparenting is different from how it was when I was growing up. During the war my father was away, training for the air force, then being a fighter pilot in the Islands. My mother and my siblings and I lived with my maternal grandparents in Papakura. My grandparents were just there, a constant part of my life until I was 10. So different.

'I went to visit Ivan today and I gave him his lunch. One of the things I notice when I visit Ivan is that when I'm with him I need to touch him.'

Dangers for grandparents

- Lego on the floor.
- Standing on wobbly stools looking into long-forgotten cupboards for long-unused toys.
- Answering difficult questions. (Tane asked me: 'Why is *Swan Lake* so noisy when the music's about swans on a lake?')
- Prescription drugs having to be in inaccessible places. This may result in your falling off a stepladder when you go to retrieve them after the children have left, but the kids are more important than your drugs. This includes alcohol.
- Boredom — preschoolers' repetitive use of the word 'Again!'
- Over-eating; the children's leftovers, and all that baking: the chocolate cakes, pikelets and cupcakes.
- Kids resetting your TV remote.
- Having to understand spelt-out words. ('What are you getting for his B-I-R-T-H-D-A-Y?') At the speed at which a daughter spells words out over the child's head, it's better than the mental workout of Sudoku.

Leautuliilagi Sauvao

A live-in teenage grandchild

'I was born in Samoa, and so was my husband. So we are what you would call a traditional Samoan family. I came to New Zealand when I was 20 years old. I married a Samoan-born Samoan here, and we have three grown-up children, all New Zealand-born. We have one grandchild, a son, from my youngest, my daughter.

'Uriah stays with us, his grandparents. He and his mother have been with us right from the start. His mother, now she lives in Auckland, with other relatives, because of her job. She's done her training and is with Qantas. She can't get a job down here in Wellington. Sometimes, when Uriah was little, he was often disobedient to us, but never to his mother. He was, and is always, very attentive to her.

'He is 15. When he first went to college, he went to St Pat's. My other daughter, my eldest, she is a teacher at St Pat's. He moved out and stayed with her, but he found that having an aunty at school is stressful. And she was, he says, too tough on him about doing all his schoolwork. So, fine, now he's back with us and he goes to Rongotai. He's happy at school, and he says he is happy here because he hasn't been told off as much as he was by his teacher aunty.

'He's the spoiled child, because he's the only grandchild. That doesn't stop us telling him off in the way our Pasifika families do. Our children have to listen, obey, do as they are told to do. When he was two or three, we went to the funeral of my father in Samoa. He was spoiled over there. Everything he cried for, he got. Now sometimes we say "No". We say: "You have to earn that. You have to work hard."

'There are positive outcomes for us about having him living here. He does the domestic work. We let him do it. He washes the dishes for us. He serves our meals when I get home from work. I work full-time. He provides the basin for us to wash our hands, and then he takes it out. He brings it back for us to rewash our hands after eating. He provides us with cups of tea and things like that. He hangs out the washing. He does the vacuuming. When we tell him to do something, it can take a long time for him to do it. It often takes about four or five calls for him to come and do his jobs. When we have community work, like tidying up the church, he comes to help us. We will be tidying the church all this coming weekend, a long holiday weekend. He will be very useful, because he is stronger than we are.

'He eats a lot, but not the food we eat. He likes palagi food. He doesn't eat bananas or taro. This is sad for us. It means we have to spend a lot of money getting food for him. He likes that junk food, and that's what his friends like. When he was little, I assisted his mother in preparing his food. Uriah doesn't do the cooking. I used to do the cooking when my husband was working, but now that my husband is retired he does it. He is always in the kitchen. He was a welder, but now he likes his garden and cooking.

'There are things about having Uriah here that annoy me. He stays on his phone all the time and on his Xbox, and he watches lots of sport on TV. It's fine to watch rugby with us, but he spends far too much time on his phone playing games. And every time he showers there is always a pile of washing. He changes his clothes all the time. He uses lots of power.

'This year I am planning to take my husband and Uriah to our family reunion in Hawaii. His mother will be working. A lot of my relatives are in Hawaii, on my mother's side. Uriah has been asking: "Have you paid our fares? Have you booked yet?" Last week was the closing date of our registration for the reunion. He can't wait to go.

'Another benefit of his staying here with us at home is that his grandfather talks to him a lot in Samoan. Uriah doesn't speak Samoan fluently. He does understand when we talk to him. He likes listening to his grandad speak Samoan, but he feels whakama when he tries to speak it himself, in case he makes a mistake in pronunciation. Last Christmas I paid the fare for two of my nephews, my sister's grandchildren, to come over. When they arrived they spoke all the time in Samoan. It was a pity for Uriah not to speak to them fluently enough in Samoan.

'I want him to speak Samoan a lot, because he is now taking Samoan for NCEA. I stress to him that he is studying for his exam, so he must use the language at home. We used to speak Samoan to him when he was little, but when he meets his Samoan cousins, the New Zealand-born ones all speak English. His mother talks to him in English all the time, so does the aunty. Our church sings hymns in four different languages: Tokelauan, Cook Islands Maori, Samoan and English. Uriah doesn't attend the afternoon service. He comes to the morning service, which is in English. Here is the irony: the college I attended in Samoan as a high-school girl, they didn't allow you to speak Samoan once you enter the gates. So I got detention and had to look for coconut beetles. (That was the punishment.)

'I'm glad he is growing up here, because this is where we are. When he was about five his mother wanted to go to live in Australia, and so she took him there but he cried every night. He wanted to come home to us, so they had to come back.

'I wish he does well at college and goes to university and gets a degree and a good job. What's he interested in? He first said a builder, then a plumber, a rugby player. Then last year he said he wants to be a PE teacher because they have a lot of holidays. Holidays! I told him teachers work seven days a week. I should know. My father was a teacher. I am a teacher!

'I've always worked. I did night-time cleaning when the kids were little, so I could be with the child during the day and my husband could look after him at night when I was at work. I used to catch the train to Wellington at one o'clock in the morning, finish the cleaning at six, and go home on the train. Then I became a part-time nurse, then I was a weekend chef at Arohata Prison. When my youngest started at the early childhood centre, I applied for teachers' college. I've taught since 1979. I hope I've set my grandson an example; he's always seen me as a hard worker.

'I am the very important person in his life. He often comes to me for help with schoolwork, or with Samoan language. He comes to me for the provision of things like clothes and food, too. The father played up on my daughter, so we said "No more" and we separated them. Uriah sees him often now. He goes there some weekends. His father doesn't support him, because he has lots of kids from other women. He has no money to spend on his son!

'We Pasifika parents always attend to our grandchildren's spiritual life.'

'I gave Uriah a trip to Los Angeles before he started secondary school. His mother and I went, too. We had a celebration of an aunt's ninetieth birthday. We went to Las Vegas by bus. He loved that. He looks up to me all the time. He enjoys my leadership roles in the church and the community. In his meetings with teachers, he likes to take me there. I don't mind any of that. I love to support him to the full.

'One of Uriah's proudest moments was his first time at Parliament, the day I got my award from Queen Elizabeth. He saw the Governor General put the medal on me when I became an Officer of the New

Zealand Order of Merit (ONZM) because of services in education to the Pasifika community. That was a day I remember my grandson being so proud. He was nine. Uriah wrote about it at primary school.

'We Pasifika parents always attend to our grandchildren's spiritual life, make sure they attend church, that they go to all the church activities. We show them that prayer is the key thing. We encourage Uriah to do his bedtime prayer, and his morning prayer when he wakes up, and grace before food. All that. It is very important. We've trained him to do this. Last Sunday when we said our family prayer, he prayed a lot longer than before. The way he structured his prayer last Sunday was the best one since he's been trying to do it from early childhood. He did it very well. I was so pleased. I said, "You have spoken well in your prayer tonight." It is in English for him. We tried to teach him to do it in Samoan, but he isn't fluent so we allow him to pray in English. It is the same with our daughters when they come. They pray in English.

'I am a lay preacher. I preach in Samoan, but I prepare images to display on the screen. He enjoys coming to listen to me. All of my family come to support me when I preach. We are together as a family then.'

♡

Penny Zino

Boys, boys, boys ... and Labradors

I interviewed Penny on the terrace of her beautiful garden, Flaxmere.
I'd been there several times previously, but always as part of the crowds
who flock there for Art in the Garden, when the garden is open to the
public and full of astonishing art. Once I had even been the judge for
the scarecrow competition. This time it was just Penny and me. There had
been a wedding in the garden the night before, and not everything
had been put back correctly. I helped Penny move a table back to where it
should be, beside the grandchildren's sandpit. We looked over the perfect

lawn, and on, through a gap in the trees to the mountains beyond. It was beautiful, peaceful, and all of it is Penny's lifelong passion.

'I never thought for one minute that my three children would all live within 20 minutes of Flaxmere, here in North Canterbury. That must be an unusual situation for grandparents. I didn't plan it that way. It just happened. My husband, John, died 22 years ago. I remember the children were all at university at the time. Mark was doing commerce at Lincoln, and Sarah was doing a PhD at Otago. Sam did landscape architecture and a Master's in Forestry. Mark came home for a year, and we sorted ourselves out, and employed a manager. The boys travelled the world, and one by one they came home. They both decided they weren't built for inside jobs, as they couldn't bear the thought of being in an office. They both wanted to farm. So we bought another place just up the road from here, in a higher-rainfall area, and that is where Sam lives. They farm in partnership, which seems to work, as they have different jobs. Sam does deer and cattle. Mark does sheep and finishing.

'Sarah finished her PhD in human nutrition and married a Dutchman, Marco Woelders. He was in charge of the oil division in Mobil. They moved around — Christchurch, Wellington, Melbourne — and then they were offered a place in head office in Singapore. I thought they could end up anywhere, but then Marco decided to buy his own business, and he bought an arm of a small transport firm in Amberley. Within a year, the owner of the biggest trucking firm in the district, GVT, asked him to buy them out. They did a merger, and after five years he bought the other half of the company they had set up. So Sarah and Marco also settled close by. Sarah produced the first grandchild for me, Tom.

'The other unusual thing that I couldn't predict was that Sarah and both my daughters-in-law, Rachael and Keri, would all produce boys. I have eight grandsons and no granddaughters. I'm not sure how I'd deal with girls now. Boys are so different from girls.

'Over the years, my life has involved a lot of babysitting for them all, probably more for Sarah's and Sam's families, than for Mark's. Rachael's parents are my next-door neighbours, so Mark and Rachael's children have their other grandparents as well. I have all of the other five children often. They all call me "Granny P". I don't like the "Granny" word much. They can just call me "P". I love being part of their lives.

'We had a huge wind a month ago, debris everywhere, devastating. To make matters worse, the garden was to open the following day for Art in the Garden. Sarah arrived with three of the children. Two of them were on the quad-bike straight away, with the trailer. They set off down the drive and started collecting all of the rubbish. Another grandchild was on the lawnmower, clearing the lawn, tidying up. I couldn't have done it on my own.

'They are practical farm kids, always making things. As all farm children do, they learnt how to drive all types of farm machinery very early, and are already competent drivers. Mark, their father, told me it's fine. "If something happened to me, they'd know how to deal with it. They'd know which lever to pull."

'My eldest grandchild has Type 1 diabetes. This has been a huge learning curve for all of us as a family. He's done very well and is on a pump now. And is he growing! He has size 14 feet and he's 6 feet 2, and he's not even 15. Henry and Ben are both dyslexic, Henry severely. This also has been not an easy thing to deal with. Our local school didn't cater for it, so both parents spent masses of time driving the boys to Rangiora to get extra help every week. The boys ended up going to boarding school when they were quite young, so they could get the help they needed. It is a matter of having to, because you are limiting your children if they can't read. It's been a huge success in both cases. The boarding-school thing is something rural children often face. I went to boarding school when I was nine! Some of the grandchildren go to the local school. Next year, there will be four at boarding school in Christchurch and four here.

'Family gatherings happen a lot, and have always been important to me. They all come here, to Flaxmere. We have barbeques, and the swimming pool is a huge attraction in the summer. Most of the neighbours come, too. My parents were amazing, how they catered for children. My father was one of three who started the ski club behind Hanmer Springs. Mum fed 30 people every Sunday night, as everyone went back to work after skiing, and thought nothing of it. I've done the same sort of thing as my parents did. Anyone who is around, I feed them. Rural people are different from city people in this way. We all have huge deep-freezers and can just pull out something. It isn't a problem, catering for lots of people.

'I also cater for everyone at Christmas. I love Christmas. I love the trimmings and the festivity, the trees, fairy lights, and all the food. We all sit around the table. I can get 16 around the dining-room table. I always have this convention that children must sit up at the table. I hate them being separated out. They might have their own end of the table, but they have to be part of it and sit there until everyone has finished. And it is fun. They all eat too much. We have a stupid tradition which started in Madeira, which is where my husband came from. Over there, they have this thing that when Christmas pudding arrives at the table, you tip the brandy over it and set it on fire, and you have to eat it straight away with the flames still on it to bring good luck for the following year! Mark is always the one tipping the brandy on. All the kids love it. Everybody dives in. The pudding looks an absolute shambles at the end of it all. Of course they don't actually eat the flames. The fire goes out before they get it near their mouths, but it is a mad, fun time around the table. Regarding Christmas presents, I tend to buy the things the children need, especially sports gear and books. Sometimes I feel presents can get too out of hand. Sometimes they are too expensive. This year I will ask Mark and Sam to forget about Christmas presents for me, and I'll suggest, "I just need you to come with a chainsaw and get rid of the dead trees!" We've had such a dry year, and so much wind. So many of the trees, even long-established ones, are dying.

'Up at Mark and Rachael's, one recent Christmas, I remember all of the children running around outside. Rachael's brother, Matthew, had come from Wellington, and he has three boys, too. So it was *all* 11 boys and the four fathers. They all played cricket, and there were five Labradors — we all have Labradors — and the Labradors played cricket, too. The Labs were very good at retrieving the balls, but not so good at letting them go! That's a Christmas I will always have in my mind. It looked so mad. All those dogs and all those boys chasing balls.

'If the parents want me to babysit, they can bring the children here. I don't want to be at their houses. There is plenty for them to do here, and plenty of beds upstairs. I don't mind how many grandchildren I have at once. Boys are very messy. I can never believe where they leave things! They climb out of their clothes and just leave them, don't they? The house always looks like a bomb site when they go. But I love it.

'Having them here does have some disadvantages. Sarah and her husband went off skiing once, and I looked after Henry, who was only 18 months at the time. One day he was in his high-chair and throwing food all around the kitchen. Ages later, I had a picture that my mother had painted, and I took it down to be reframed. I told the guy it needed cleaning. It had a few fly-spots, I thought! The next day he phoned me and said it wasn't fly spots: it was food! I thought: "You little toad, Henry. I know where that came from!"

'I read the old favourite books to them — Beatrix Potter, Margaret Mahy, Roald Dahl, to mention a few. They haul them off the shelves. They all love cooking, especially pikelets, which are instantly in their tummies. I do have a few rules about the table. They have to sit up, eat up, not get down until everyone else has finished. And there's another rule: they do their homework here straight after afternoon tea, and before dinner. The idea is to get it done before they are too tired. Once it's done, they can go into the garden.

'There is so much garden here, and so many of the things they get up to are the same activities we got up to when we were children. They love building huts. Huts are everywhere. Underground huts, tree huts, different kinds of huts, in different locations. All the trees that were here when my children were little we have since taken out and replaced with others, but the grandchildren all keep building huts! We have saws, nails, bits of wood. I remember one father of the boys saying he could never, ever move from where he is, because he'd have to spend so much time pulling down huts before selling! They love making boats out of the stems of flax flowers, as well, and that can absorb many hours.

'As you get older, you get more interested in family history.'

'When they are here, they can go into the garden in the dark, too. I have a string of torches, and six big battery-operated, portable spotlights. I have them because the garden is often hired as an event venue. The children love the spotlights. They play a lot at night in the summer, games like Kick the Tin, Hide and Seek. They are such lucky kids.

'We have sandpits, diggers, trucks for the younger ones. And I encourage them in lots of sport when they are a little older. They play rugby, and cricket, of course. Besides the team sports, there are motorbikes and cycling. All of the grandchildren have their own motorbikes. Their parents have been so sensible; they have had outside instructors, usually in the school holidays, to instruct lots of farm children from around here. Boys learn from an outsider better than from their parents. Mark has built motorbike courses, which are hair-raising! They are careful grandchildren, but they do go fast, and I don't like that much.

'I love watching them playing all their sports. I spend a lot of time, in all weathers, on the sidelines of a rugby game. Being a gardener I'm not put off by weather. In summer I watch cricket with Ben. Jack's into tennis, and Tom's into rowing. I watch them all. I drive to Twizel for the rowing. Tom's team won a gold in the South Island Schools Championship last year, and the same team won a bronze for their year in the Maadi Cup, so that was pretty clever. Tom was in the Eight, and it was his first year up. That's exciting. They all ski, of course, and water-ski. It means I do a lot of driving. I seem to spend my life in the car! You have to, to support the grandchildren.

'Now that some of them are older, they are being taught to shoot. There is a clay pigeon set up on one of the terraces, and that is another skill that will be life-long. They are all mad keen fishermen, and I have bought every grandson his own rod. Jack and Ollie are very good. I have a place in the Sounds, and we go there in the summer holidays, and all love fishing and camping. What they have in common is that they all love the outdoors.

'All of the grandchildren have their own motorbikes.'

'For their tenth birthdays I have a day with each of the grandchildren on their own. We do whatever they want to do. It was my idea. I just wanted to do something special for each child. It's interesting that most of them choose something to do with either fishing or animals. They want to go to Orana Park, or swimming with dolphins, or whale-watching. It's a whole day out, usually a long drive to get to wherever we have to go to. One time I took two children at the same time, because their birthdays were close together and I knew they were both going to choose the same thing. So we went to Kaikoura and went fishing. We had a great day.

'I go in to Christchurch a lot, to the theatre and the orchestra. I haven't managed to persuade the boys to do that with me yet! They aren't interested. Maybe if I had a granddaughter …

'We had a bit of earthquake damage here, and I've had painters and plasterers in, and that was quite good for me, because it motivated me to go through all of our photos and papers. I'm busy making little piles for everyone, trying to identify the people in photographs. I have masses of stuff to go through. I do this for the grandchildren. As you get older, you get more interested in family history. I'd like to write about the family, too, for the grandchildren. My grandfather was killed at Gallipoli. He was only 26. He left New Zealand before my father was born, so my father never saw his father. We have his diary and all of my grandfather's letters to my grandmother. They've been made into a book and copied for everyone. I think those documents of family history are important. I hope I get around to doing more of it. We can't put these projects off.

'I hope some of the boys will be part of the family business. Farms tend to go on in a family, because from a young age children are part of it. They help with all of the jobs. These grandchildren are rural kids. They love the animals and anything to do with motorbikes. But they are all different from each other, too. I can already see that one of them won't farm. I think the difference between rural and urban children is becoming more marked. I worry that urban children are now so technology-based they don't seem to see the outside world.

'In 2016, I will have been here at Flaxmere 50 years. The grandchildren have seen the garden evolve. Will they love gardening? One of them is already quite knowledgeable. Son Sam is very interested in trees, and he's been teaching the Latin names of trees to Jack and Ollie. I think what they know is amazing. Ben also is very good in the garden. He takes a pole-saw and is a tremendous help in sawing off branches that have splits lengthwise after big snowfalls. We always take the quad-bike and the trailer, and off we go. He is such a help. None of them is good at weeding, but I don't expect anyone to be good at weeding. I haven't managed to lure them into growing vegetables as yet. They all have vegetable gardens at their own homes. For me, the garden is all about design, creating vistas and, most important of all, the change of seasons. We are so lucky to live in a place with the change of seasons; it is a huge part of the joy of living.

'I hope these children grow up with a broad concept of life. You see life and death all the time on a farm. Our rural children understand that. I grew up on a farm. I drove a tractor when I was eight. I'm like my father. He was attached to the land. I feel like a tree that has put down roots. That's what farms do to people. Your roots go down. You feel good there. You feel you belong. You don't have that feeling in a city.

'I hope I've taught them all the ability to work hard in whatever they choose to do in life; I don't mind what they do. I just like to see them make an effort and have a go. I also hope I've given them a love of the outdoors and the plant world, and of course the wildlife that goes with all that. I hope they get these messages by seeing these values in me, by having shared Flaxmere with me.'

♡

Mary and Phillip Sutton

❧

'It's the crisis times that are hard'

'When we were starting a family, I saw a beautiful cradle, wooden, on rockers, Danish-style, stained wood, gingham tent over it. I wanted it, but we couldn't afford it. We went into the shop. My task was to keep the shop assistant busy while Phillip measured it up. He made one, just like the one in the shop. I made the gingham covers. We still have it, and everyone has been in it.'

'Everyone' includes their three girls, and all of the grandchildren and all of the nieces and nephews. All of the children and grandchildren live in the same town as Mary and Phillip. Middle daughter, Joanna, has special needs. Two of Joanna's three children have special needs. Mary is the go-to person who supports them.

Mary: 'The first of Joanna's children, my first grandchild, Jacob, was such a placid baby. Joanna prepared well for him, but motherhood was a huge shock for her. She got depressed, and we had her and Jacob living here for a time because of that. I cared for Jacob. This is why I have such a strong bond with him. I was doing child psychotherapy training at the time, and I remember writing up my big case studies while Jacob lay on the carpet, smiling.

'Catherine, our youngest daughter, was at home then, too, and she did a lot of looking after him as well. I knew Joanna was getting better when she said "I'll do that", and she took over the caring. I still had a lot to do with him when he was little. I used to take him to Playcentre one day a week. That was fun. When they left our home and set up on their own, I was so upset. It was grief. I hadn't realised how much that attachment had grown. It was right that he went with his mum, but it was terrible for me.

'With our help, Joanna could cope with one child, but things were much more complicated after Caitlin was born. She was a difficult child from the beginning, but we coped. However, when Joanna was pregnant again, oh dear, we had a huge row in Farmers. She was looking at baby equipment, and I thought, "What's going on here?" I said, "Joanna, are you pregnant again?" She said, "Yes." And I just lost it. Completely. I've never done such a thing before. In the middle of Farmers. Joanna just said, "God will provide." At that stage they were involved with a church. I banged my hands down on the pushchair, and I said, "That's all very well, but at the moment He's providing through us!" Joanna stomped off, and I spent the next half-hour looking for her in that huge shop. That was awful.

'We are the advocates for these grandchildren, and we have had to fight very hard for them, especially when Joanna's marriage failed. It ended up with us having to go to court to get custody of them. Both financially and emotionally, it was really hard.

'We had Jacob living with us for a year when he was eight, and then he went back to his mum. He is now 19. He has Asperger's, mild depression and anxiety. He is a big worry for us at the moment. He's living in a hostel, where his father, who also has special needs, lives. We thought that would be a good thing, but his father can be negative with him. We are having a lot to do with Jacob now. Because he is quite paranoid, it is difficult to get him to access help. I am doing a lot of work trying to get other agencies on board with him, but we get to a certain point and then he will say he doesn't want anything to do with them. He trusts us absolutely. I spend sleepless nights over Jacob.

'We have had Caitlin living with us, too. That was extremely difficult. She is 16. She is now in care, and we are happy with the care she is getting. It has been a long road to get to there. We still see her often. We are her legal guardians, because we felt she would need an advocate to ensure that her care was being managed properly, but when she is 17 CYFs will discharge her, so that's a worry in the pipeline.

'Because of the special needs of the children and Joanna, a lot of the contact we have with them is around helping. It's hard to just say, "Come round and let's hang out." We feed Jacob good food, because he's not good at providing for himself. When he was at school he made a Cape Cod chair, and we've always said he could sell it on Trade Me. So, recently he's been working with Phillip — Poppa — painting the chair. That's been pleasurable. We both noticed that when he had that project, doing the chair, Jacob became more normal, less paranoid. Always at the back of my mind I'm thinking: "Now this will be good for Jacob to complete a task, to work with Poppa." It's always there, that need to help, which I don't have to do with the others.

'Looking after Jo and her family is the main focus of our retirement. Phillip wishes that it wasn't. He feels he could let it go more than me. It does keep us both very busy. I have ambivalence, too. It's hard not to cross over the line and be helping with resentment. I don't want that. I feel a tremendous feeling of responsibility, more so than Phillip.

'One night we were watching TV, in our nightclothes, just before bed. The phone rang. It was Joanna saying this thing has fallen off the shower and she can't turn the water off. She's in a Housing Corp house. There's no one to call at that hour of night except us. So Phillip got

dressed, packed his tools. I didn't change. I just put on my dressing gown. I took towels to mop up the water. By the time we arrived, there was a flood.

'We two are more accepting now. We know everyone has difficulties in life. You just get on with it. It's to do with our stage in life. I now accept it when Jacob refuses the help agencies I'm trying to arrange for him. It's age that makes me more accepting. And I realise now that what we can do for them is limited. For Joanna, we put in so much just to try to make it good enough. And I know that, even with all of that help, those children haven't had the same experiences as our other grandchildren.

'Christine is our eldest child. She's got two girls, Isabella and Emma. I was privileged to be at the birth of both of them. Christine asked if I would come in. That was an amazing experience. They are lovely, bright children. Catherine has had her babies late. She's in her forties and she has four-year-old Emily and a nearly one-year-old, Charlotte. They haven't been easy babies, either. We have been helping them as well. Her husband is English, and so he has no family here to help. Catherine's children have digestive problems. Emily vomited her way through year one, and was hospitalised twice for failing to thrive. Charlotte has the same difficulty — she is so tiny — but so far, so good. We all thought about how to make it possible for Catherine to go back to work, because she loved her job, but when we worked it out, if we had looked after her children so she could work, we also had to look after Jo and her children. We just couldn't do it.

'On birthdays and Christmas we all get together. Jo's children have a strong sense of family and love their cousins. Nicky, Joanna's third child, loves coming to be with Grandma and Poppa, and sometimes she stays here with her cousins. We have seven grandchildren now, so the gatherings are big.

'We've had wonderful holiday times. Friends at Coromandel let us use their big house with all the children and grandchildren. And a friend lives on a lifestyle block at Kaipara Flats, and we do house-sitting there, and everyone stays. The grandchildren love the animals, sheep, goats, geese, chickens, dogs, cats. It was amazing to see Jacob there, how he became more grounded. He'd go and stand in the paddock when the stars were coming out and watch them. He loved it.

'I have learnt that love is not enough.'

'The kids love Phillip — Poppa. He teases them and plays with them, especially on holiday. Once, at Kaipara Flats, the kids went to get the eggs with Poppa. The hens weren't laying, so Poppa put an egg where the hens were, with Isabella's name on it. Well, she was delighted. She couldn't understand how the hen had laid that egg just for her. She carried it so carefully. And one time Poppa was fed-up with all the kids being inside, so he told them that they could count the sheep in the paddock, and the one who got the right answer for how many sheep there were could get a couple of dollars. That kept them busy all afternoon.

'My friends give me support and appreciation. I have a friend who has a special-needs boy, and that's great support. I have a walking group where we walk and talk, and share our lives. It's not a heavy thing. It's just great fun. I think about my health. I go to the gym. I eat well. You just have to look after yourself, because we can't help anyone if we aren't well. I'm more careful now about the kids' bugs. When we were driving Emily to preschool because Charlotte was so delicate with the vomiting, we got all of the bugs. And we don't get over them as fast as we used to. We are getting older. Phillip's memory isn't so good now. He gets tired. He needs to be my priority, too. I do get exhausted. Catherine is mindful of our energy levels, which is good. It's the crisis times that are hard.

'I love my grandchildren. They are just delightful. With grandchildren you can be a child again. We are so lucky having littlies around at our age. You forget how exciting the world is, and they show you. I enjoy seeing their lives, feeling their energy, seeing the world through their eyes. I was a teacher first, then a child psychotherapist. Maybe I was just so busy as a mother that I didn't have time to think. But now I make sure I savour the special moments.

'I have trouble saying "No" to the family. I'm learning, but it is hard to say "No" to the grandchildren. In hindsight we have perhaps been too helpful. I worry about the future, when we won't be here. There will come a time, soon, when we won't be able to do all the things we now do. I have to come to an acceptance of that. That's why we want these other agencies involved with the grandchildren who need care. I have learnt that love is not enough.'

♡

Ridha

Yolande Palmer

❧

The leisure to love the 6am baby

Yolande and her two sons are busy running two eateries in Mt Albert: Chinoiserie, a fun place selling Taiwanese street food; and L'Oeuf, a gourmet café. (Since we spoke, they have opened a third café, Kiss Kiss, in Balmoral.) She lives in a house near the cafés with Jasper, her younger son, his partner, Celeste, and their six-month-old baby, Casmir.

There's no conflict about living all together, no conflict about who does the cooking, washing, cleaning, etc. 'It's very easy co-habitation. My son does all the cooking, of course. We aren't very house-proud, so that makes it easy. The fanaticism for cleaning stays in the cafés. It's a typical situation: if you look in our kitchen, you wouldn't believe we are foodies. We don't even have decent knives and forks!

'I work four days a week, where I live in, looking after adults. It's amazing seeing the change in Casmir every time I return from those days of work. Every time I can see some way that he has grown. Being a grandparent you are more aware of the process. You know that each step is part of a chain. At the moment he is on all fours and he's rocking backwards and forwards. Maybe when I come back next time he will have taken off into crawling. I don't remember noticing those milestones when I had my boys. It was too frenetic.

'My leisure time is now mine, and I guard it jealously. I'm catching up with everything I couldn't do in those 35 years of married life. I will be 60 soon, and I have my time for me. I do the flowers in the cafés for the kids. My flowers in L'Oeuf are more like installations. I use organic lichens, and fungus. I make light-boxes. I started that at Chinoiserie because I wanted something warm on the tables. I put petals up against glass, and then place a light behind it to make a glowing object. It's fascinating, but I'm trying to slow down a little bit.'

When Celeste announced her pregnancy, she was the floor manager, training the staff. Then the baby came and everything changed. Life became, and still is, Yolande says, a celebration.

Yolande thought back to the time she had her own babies. She had thought that having babies was the most important thing she wanted to do in life, but 'it was a shock when it happened. I am creative, and coping with two boys close together in age put me in conflict. There was no more time for me, for my creativity. So I struggled with those first five years. When I knew a grandchild was coming, I didn't know what my response would be, because I didn't want to lose my autonomy. I always said I was so over it with being a mum that I wasn't looking forward to going back to that space. But now it is completely different, because I can dip in and dip out of it. It isn't the 24-hour need. I don't like dependence.

'Celeste, my daughter-in-law, is different from me in that all she wants is to be with the baby. So I haven't had to lose my time for me. I am so happy that my daughter-in-law doesn't feel that conflict between mothering and being her own person. There are no conflicts with how Celeste is bringing him up. She's the most beautiful mother. He is such a happy boy. She has never asked me to look after him, because she is so besotted with doing it all herself. That's perfect for me. I'm not crazy about little babies.

'The household has a perfect routine. I'm an early-morning person. My son knows I'm well and truly awake then. So I get the baby at 6am in my bed. This little bundle comes in. I have the most delicious cuddles. He gets tucked in — or he used to, but now that he is six months old I have all this stuff around to entertain him. He's very active. But I remember those first three months. This beautiful little bundle coming in. I kissed the top of his head, smelling him. I talked to him. I talk to babies a lot. I think in a way I might have maybe made my son and Celeste relaxed about the nonsense you have to do when you are with children. Grandparents know how to have a non-stop conversation with a little baby. Grandparents know how to be children with them. Our children have to learn they won't lose their dignity by doing it. You have to be totally uninhibited. I think they are learning that from me.

'Grandparents know how to have a non-stop conversation with a little baby.'

'I've set up a stereo in my bedroom. I went into an op shop and found a lot of Rattle and Rhyme CDs. I'll only put on something I can bear to listen to myself. Casmir could be very in-tune with sound. If I put on the noisy Nutrimix blender, he cries. When I put on music, he really listens. If he starts to get bored with my talking to him, I sing to him. I can engage him for quite a while. I sing nursery rhymes. I know so many nursery rhymes that I didn't realise I knew! I didn't sing them to my kids.

'I took my children to France when they were little, because we wanted them to be bilingual. Their father is French. And so I realised that nursery rhymes and fairy tales are a really big part of your culture.

We don't realise how much we cross-reference all the time. Before I went to France, I had to learn French nursery rhymes so I could do that part of their education. I had a gap without the English ones. So quaint, aren't they?

> Where have you been all the day, Billy Boy, Billy Boy?
> I've been walking all day with my charming Nancy Grey.
> She's a good girl but cannot leave her mother!

I was just lucky in that op shop to have found these old ones. They are beautiful old ditties.

'He's too young for stories yet. I can't wait. I already have a little library going. When the time comes, it will be a big, big pleasure. He will have a bilingual experience, because my son is more dedicated to this than his father was. Every time he picks up little Casmir, he speaks to him in French, and also in the car we play the French nursery rhymes so that is subliminal for him. I also have a French niece. She's married a Kiwi guy, and she's here now, just down the road.

'Living with the baby allows for a deep bond. We all used to have a real daily deep bond with babies generations ago, when Grandma was living right there, in the house. I had no grandparents in my own life when I was a child, but I did have a model of the perfect grandmother. She was my ex-husband Phillippe's mother. She was gorgeous. We moved over there, stayed in the house with her. Jasper was a baby, and he has always woken early. She would be waiting at the bottom of the stairs for him to come down, and Jasper would then have this very privileged hour or two in the kitchen with her, preparing his little breakfast. Everything had to be proper. Her being in the kitchen with him when it was just her and him, has it influenced him? He is now surrounded by food preparation and kitchens, so maybe it has. Her rituals — she had this knife that was her knife, which she spread butter with. It was so worn-down, it was like a needle. You'd wait for her to try to spread the butter with that needle. She'd chop the bread into little soldiers, and give them to him. I remember the smells of her kitchen. Jasper took Celeste there a while ago — Phillippe's sister is now living in the house — and he told me that the smells were the same: lardons, thyme. I remember that she made all her own jams, like plum jam with cinnamon in it. She used simple ingredients, never any more than five ingredients in a dish. There were always stews slowly cooking. So much time was spent in food preparation then, in selecting food at the market, the consideration that went into just buying a leek.

'I think I'd love to be a bit slower, to be the sort of grandparent that my children had with their father's mother. She was at that stage in life where she was totally serene and "here now". She gave that sort of presence and that sort of appreciation to what she was doing. I'm not that sort of grandmother, but I think that is enormously valuable. I wish modern children today had that serenity in their lives. I think that serenity might come to me when I'm retired. I'm too hungry for life still, right now, to be the serene grandmother, but I'm happy I saw that, and saw the beauty of it.

'The shared dream for both my sons, Jasper and Ludovic, is to buy a plot of land and have a whole lot of separate dwellings on it, and for us all to live there with all of the grandchildren, and grow food for the cafés. "All" means Celeste's parents, too. The sons feel strongly that they want to put the older generation and the younger generation together. Celeste's mum says, "Won't it be great when we are looking after all the grandbabies?"

'How do I feel about lots of them running around? I know I am going to get them. Celeste is pregnant again. How would I feel about living that kind of country life? The older I get, the more simple are my needs. All I want is a garden, books and music. There must be nothing more beautiful for a grandparent than to tell a child to take a bowl out into the garden and pick a bowl of peas.

'All in all, my life now is a mystery. I'm a happy-on-my-own person, yet I'm living with my family. I guard my independence, yet adore looking after my grandson. I am totally blessed, and blissed. It is powerful stuff, this beauty, this present I've been given.'

♡

Te Maari Gardiner, Tuwharetoa

'Keeping the old people with me'

Te Maari has strong childhood memories of her grandmother arriving on the bus from Tauranga to stay for a few months. 'She was formal, dignified, always dressed in black, speaking entirely in Maori. She seemed ancient to me, and of another world. She wasn't the sort of grandmother you clamber all over, and sit on their laps. I would never sit on her knee — but how I love it now, when six of my own grandchildren clamber all over me!'

Te Maari would sit beside her grandmother, and watch her nod off in her chair, then she'd creep up really close to her and almost touch her chin. She'd keep her finger steady, a little distance away from her chin, and slowly trace the pattern of her grandmother's moko kawai. 'It mesmerised me. I was absolutely intrigued by it. And I just held that thought in the back of my head all through my childhood. Her moko kawai was an inspiration for me. It was something that I knew I would do eventually.

'I did it in 1999, as a way of keeping those old people with me from the previous century, and bringing them into the new century. It is a combination of the patterns of two kuia, some from my grandmother on my dad's side, but also part of it is the woman I was named after, Te Maari. And there's a piece there that is just for me.

'It's about opening doors again, because I have seven grand-daughters at the moment, maybe more to come, and to me it was about a door that was closed to my generation. A few of us consciously made the decision to whack that door right open again and reclaim all of these practices that our generation had lost. Our parents had them and took them for granted, but we were directed to have a good Pakeha education. That was a way forward. Economically, that was the way you looked after your family. You can't blame your parents for that. But we did lose a lot of things.'

Te Maari's 86-year-old mum and 89-year-old dad still live in the house that her mother's mother lived in. 'We used to help her drive her cows down the road to the milking shed, through swamp, sometimes with water up to our chests in flood times. She was a strong, independent woman. We were in awe of her.'

Te Maari and her five siblings look after their parents. 'I have two sisters and their families, who live close to my parents. They are the eyes and hands right there. Those of us who live a little bit further out, we do a weekend every six weeks. But, then again, we can be called at a moment's notice. We will drop anything. They are the highest priority.

'My own children still have their grandparents, so their children have their great-grandparents, mokopuna tuarua. My house up here, at Raurimu, out towards Ruapehu, has plenty of space and one very big room, so lots of family gatherings are held at my place to take the pressure off Mum and Dad. I consciously bought the property so that if any of the kids wanted to come and build a house there, they could. I guess at some sort of level it was there, that natural drive, the thing grandparents do, providing for the children. I didn't think too much about it. I just knew I needed a bit of space and to make it available for them all.'

Te Maari has four children, two boys and two girls, and 12 grandchildren, seven girls and five boys. The eldest is 11 and the youngest is only a few months old. Her husband has his 12 grandchildren as well. His are a little bit older. He has three great-grandchildren.

'I'd like them to have a social conscience.'

'So all together we have quite a haul. They all live within arm's reach, which is the way we all like it. They come to me for advice. They always come and talk. We make decisions at whanau level.

'I love the kids, absolutely love them. I see most of them every day. I enjoy a hands-on role in their lives. My role is to support their parents, whichever way I can. I will always be there, always. If there are difficult times, like marriage break-ups, I am there to support in whatever way is called for. My priority always is the grandkids, for them to be safe and happy. I need them to be stable, and I work to make sure they are not impacted too heavily by what their parents are doing. It's a bit like a safety-net. We've had Nate for such a long time, five years, and his little sister for a couple of years. Nate is nine now. My husband and I have brought him up. He's just gone back to his father this year.'

Te Maari is an artist and illustrator. I have, and treasure, copies of some Margaret Mahy stories that she has illustrated. There is always drawing equipment and paper and paints at her house, and her mokopuna love drawing.

'When we were growing up, we just didn't have the scrapbooks and the paper. We used to take turns at using the back of the calendar page when the month was up. We opened brown paper bags and drew on them.' Her younger son and his wife are both artists, and their daughter, aged six, can already draw well. 'Another grandchild, Seth, will just sit and do nothing but draw. I remember I was like that as a kid.'

She takes them to the marae whenever appropriate. They've all been through kohanga reo. 'My own children went through kohanga reo, too, except the two eldest, because kohanga reo wasn't around for them. My children all have a good level of fluency. I've let the parents make the decisions about what schools their kids go to. They can pick up Maori without having it taught to them at school. When the kids come to me, they can speak both Maori and English. I give them the language and the Maori way of doing things.

'We have to stand back a lot and let our children make the decisions regarding their children, but I think that we have a very open and free relationship. We talk about everything and anything. I think we can influence them in a softer way, so the parents end up thinking it is their idea.

'I have my own spiritual beliefs, which I pass on to the children. It's a natural way to think. You have a responsibility to keep everything in balance. I don't sit down and lecture them. It's just the way we do things.' She shows the young ones how to connect to a simple appreciation of harvest, to Rongo-marae-roa, when they are gardening. She tells them about gardening by the moon, maramataka, and the rhythms of Nature. 'This is what Maori spirituality was. I told my children they could decide if they wanted to be Catholics, and my grandmother was in their ear until they all agreed to be baptised! That was fine.'

The Tuwharetoa Festival is a big thing for all of the local schools. The kids love participating, and Te Maari is always there, watching the kids. Supporting them around all of the Maori cultural events is important to her. 'I want them to be comfortable in both worlds, so that they can make their own life choices from a position of confidence on both sides. I had to work on that for myself, so that's why I gave my own children the opportunity to be strong in their Maori side. That is a role I take seriously.

'I am also passionate about the environment. I like to take the kids out into the bush, talking about the trees and the birds. I love taking them down to the lake or the river. My husband takes them fishing. It

Nana and me, Callay, aged 4

This is me and kokor.

Frida - aged 6

hurts me when I see children mistreat animals. I don't like it. To me, having them take care of animals is really big, because it helps them to take care of other things. I love to see that in the kids. And they love it — feeding the chooks, collecting the eggs, feeding the pigs. It's not a chore for them. The kids love to come out here just to let loose, to run around, get dirty.

'We were outside kids; they are inside kids. PlayStations, technology and TV keep the kids inside. When the kids come home to us for the weekend, the TV doesn't go on unless there's some movie they specifically want to watch. Otherwise we are outside. That's the biggest difference between my childhood and theirs. We didn't have electricity when I was very small. We were outside from after breakfast, all day. We only came in to eat. We were allowed to wander, find tadpoles and birds' nests. We managed to fill the day, but kids don't do that now. They have to be coaxed out of the house. They almost seem to be in need of direction.

'Even my eldest daughter's kids, who live in the country, don't experience the rural life like we did. Her husband milks cows on a big incorporation farm, so there are OSH regulations about the kids not being allowed to be out there doing stuff the way we did. They're restricted to their little area. We were brought up being unrestricted. We rode horses, played in culverts and under bridges. We didn't think about safety. I probably wouldn't let my grandchildren now do what we did then, though.

'In future I'd like them to be well-rounded, contributing people who care about others, who care about the environment. I'd like them to have a social conscience. I'd like them to be confident in making life choices that suit their personalities and ambitions. I just want the best for them.'

Te Maari doesn't have time to do her art at the moment. 'In terms of big stuff, I need to focus, and I haven't got the concentrated time right now. But,' she says, 'I am always scribbling. I have plans to get back into it.'

What grandchildren give us

- A new name.
- A new lease on life.
- A belief in our own goodness. They make us full of tenderness, concern, responsibility, love.
- A second chance. We can do better what we didn't do well the first time round.
- A chance to reinvent ourselves.
- A refreshed memory. We remember the lyrics of songs we sang as lullabies years ago.
- A chance to be eccentric.
- An excuse to play Simon and Garfunkel, The Beatles, Pete Seeger, The Beach Boys, even Peter, Paul and Mary in the car.
- The opportunity to dance to loud music in the afternoon.
- A helpdesk for our computer and network woes.
- A reason to make up silly words, silly stories.
- The pleasure in seeing our children as parents.
- The pleasure of chatting to other grannies and grandads.
- The opportunity to hoard, and to renew the dressing-up box.
- The knowledge that it is never too late to fall in love again.
- Contagious diseases.

Stacey Naish

Showing them resilience

Penny sent her mother, Stacey, a photo of son Arthur's toe and asked, 'What's this?' Stacey is a trained nurse, and works a couple of days a week at the health centre. 'Impetigo,' she diagnosed promptly. 'A school sore. You need to get him to the doctor.' But Penny was busy, so off went Stacey to pick her grandson up from school and take him to the doctor's. It's only a two-and-a-half-hour drive there to Black Estate Winery at Waipara from Akaroa, where Stacey lives and works!

'So I picked him up from school and took him to the doctor, then I stayed the night and took all the kids to school in the morning. I had the whole day with them yesterday, and I just loved it, because Arthur's often at school when I'm there working at the winery.' She works at the winery some of the time, too.

'I made a decision when the first grandchild, Toby, was born that it would be either grandchildren or golf. It couldn't be both. Any days other than my working days, if they need me I'm happy to hop in the car and whiz up to Waipara. I feel privileged they ask me. I just do whatever they want.

'Campbell is our eldest son. He married Briar, and they have three sons: Toby, 11, Felixstowe, nine, and Archy, seven. When Campbell was growing up, he was always wanting a brother. Three years after he was born, I had twin girls, so we got him a Labrador! Campbell is now in seventh heaven with his own boys. He coaches rugby and cricket, and they are always outside throwing balls. Briar is a marvellous mum. Penelope and Joanna are my twin girls. Penny married Nicholas, and they have Sylvia, eight, who is into horse-riding, and Arthur, who is six. Joanna married Alistair, and they won't have children; that's their choice. She's a career woman, so she and Alistair are a brilliant aunt and uncle.

'I know Toby well, because I used to look after him. I looked after Felixstowe when Archy was born. After that they moved to Auckland, which is where we had moved from to give our kids a country lifestyle! I go up there to babysit if the parents want to go away for the weekend, and if they give me enough warning. On one visit I had my greatest grandmother outing. As Campbell went out the door, he said, "The Twenty20 is on: New Zealand versus England. The boys would love to go to that." I'm always up for a challenge, so I went down to the Ticketek at New World and got great tickets, and we went off to Eden Park. I just said to them: "I'm worried about you boys disappearing in this huge place. I'm going to be a nervous grandmother, so you have to look after me today." They did! The boys were marvellous. It was fun. I was so proud of myself and of them.

'Here in Akaroa, we have 35 acres for them all to run around on, plenty of land for ball sports. They pitch tents. Things are dumped all over the floor. I use the house like a bach when they are all here. I'd rather they didn't write on the walls, of course, but I'm relaxed about the mess. I just love it.

'They like coming here because of the big view of the sea. It's so peaceful, a different place from Auckland. They come up the drive, in the door, and they go straight out onto this big lawn and they stare at the sea, and then they settle.

'I looked after Sylvia when she was smaller. I went there one day a week to help out. It was lovely, but then they moved to Waipara. It was great when we had the flat in the centre of Christchurch. How I miss that flat! It was halfway between the winery and Akaroa. I had this vision that I'd be able to come up to town and the kids could meet us there, and I'd take them to the museum and we'd bike around. It's one of the losses from the earthquake. It's a long way now for them to come to us — a five-hour return trip.

'The first earthquake happened when Rod was in Akaroa and I was staying overnight in the Christchurch flat for a book launch. (Oh, yes, it was one of yours, Janice!) With the second, bigger quake in February, Penny and Rod and the two children were in our flat. The kids were upstairs. Nicholas was in Australia, so there was no one at home at the vineyard. The flat was right opposite the church that came down, killing three people. Sylvia was on the bed. A big piece of furniture fell, just missing her. Arthur slept through it all. Luckily, Rod was able to get Penny's car out. Penny had to drive across the Waimakariri River with the kids, not knowing what she was going to find at home. A policeman told her, "Get north as fast as you can."

'Since then, of course, there is a heightened awareness. We never go out without our phones. We always have torches. One night in Akaroa, Sylvia leapt out of bed during an aftershock, very upset. I'm more aware now of what could happen, and it isn't just concern about earthquakes. I could be walking along with a grandchild and a car could come and knock us over. In the country, kids are in the car a lot, and there are huge trucks on the roads. Any accident can happen. When I have the boys and we are out and about and they go to their loo and I go to mine, I think of abductions. I'm so relieved to see them when they re-emerge. In Auckland when I wait at home for the kids after school, it's the same; the sense of relief when I see them.

'I am a great believer in resilience, and I do believe it is not what happens to children but how they cope that is important. Last Easter,

Sylvia, Arthur and I learnt the lesson of resilience. I was up in Waipara, about to bring the children back for a few days, and I had not realised just how much rain had fallen on Banks Peninsula. By the time we got to Little River, we learnt that the road to Akaroa might be closed by slips and fallen debris. It was either turn around for a two-hour trip all the way back, or hope and go on. The kids and I decided we were going on. I told them we had to be resilient and, although we could get out of the car and had lots of water, there wasn't going to be any entertainment. The iPad remained in the boot. They were amazing. We saw huge waterfalls and slips. I was so proud of their awareness, composure and ability to see it as an adventure. Needless to say, we arrived safely and all good.

'Akaroa is more the family base now. When Arthur and Sylvia come to stay, they always want the big bedroom with the king-size bed. They often stay here without their parents. Sylvia goes through my jewellery and scarves. I do baking with them; pikelets and gingerbread. I love children's movies like *Puss in Boots* — I must have watched it five times — and *Badjelly the Witch*. The kids love being with Rod. He plays Peter, Paul and Mary CDs to them in the car!

'Grandparents get a second chance at closeness with children.'

'I'm not a strict grandmother. The only thing I ever say is "Sit up straight at the dinner table and use your knife and fork, because one day you may be invited to Buckingham Palace." That was fine until recently, when Sylvia answered: "Actually, I don't want to go, Granny."

'I try to give them a bit of humour, too. I'm not a fount of knowledge. I dish out plenty of encouragement and positive reinforcement. Not hard: I think they are all wonderful.

'My mother was dead at 64. I didn't have either parent by the time I was 40, so my kids don't remember their maternal grandparents well. Rod's parents were great as grandparents. They lived at Kakanui, and took the kids fishing and made them shoes out of seaweed. Real old-fashioned stuff.

'Rod and I and Nicholas and Penny are all involved in Black Estate. It's a family business: three vineyards, a restaurant and a tasting room. Nicholas is a good winemaker. I have no expectations that the grandchildren will be interested in the business, but I know it will get into their blood. When they are older, they will either work at the vineyard or have to find a job elsewhere, because they won't be allowed to be lying around idle and indolent. You just give the children an example of a work ethic; this is how things are done. I think they learn from our example. Sylvia loves to help in the restaurant, and she's good at it, but she's told her dad she's not going to be making wine. She's going to be a vet.

'We used to think that every generation would do better than their parents, but not anymore. I'm concerned about the health of the river where Penny takes them for picnics. I wish they'd halve the number of cows in the paddocks. I'm concerned about climate change and inequality. We lived in a time when we never felt we had more or less than anyone else. I worked at South Auckland Hospice and saw how the dice are stacked against poor people. We left Auckland when our kids were school kids, because we saw already the ostentatiousness of modern life. I worry about kids having relationships only with their computer. I bemoan the fact that children don't walk or bike to school anymore. The health of kids in general isn't good now.

'There are improvements, too. Fathers today are much more involved. When I had a three-year-old *and* twins *and* ran a delicatessen on Greenwoods Corner, The Onion Skin, Rod went off to do a business degree! But today's young fathers do spend time with their kids.

'I have more time for my grandchildren than I had for my kids. And I get so much out of it! When I'm with them, I see the world as it is for them. It makes me not so selfish. I take more interest in my surroundings, in everything really. Grandparents get a second chance at closeness with children.'

♡

Shewaynesh and Awthash Hailu

Awthash and Shewaynesh Hailu, and Faiza Hanslo

Being a new kind of grandparent

I met Faiza Hanslo, and Shewaynesh Hailu and her mother, Awthash, at the United Muslims Migrants Association centre in Auckland, where the two younger women both work. They are strong, independent women who are the heads of their respective households.

Shewaynesh manages the Women's Empowerment Group at May Road School. She speaks English, Arabic, Amharic and Tigrean. She came here 18 years ago, leaving Awthash in a Sudanese camp. They had fled the war in Ethiopia. Her mother and two brothers arrived here 10 years later. Some of Awthash's six grandchildren are still in Sudan. Shewaynesh said, 'We are settled here now. My younger daughter is 16 and doing well at school, and my older daughter has twin boys, just newborn. They were baptised last week.

'It was so hard to get my mother out here. She came in the family quota. When she finally arrived at Auckland, she was so happy, so emotional. There were two grown-up granddaughters for her to meet, one aged 20 and one 10.

'When I saw the end result of having a grandmother in the family, I was glad I had done that hard work to make her join us. The result is to make everyone more happy. Having a grandmother around makes everything different. The feeling is different. My children act differently when there are family around. I see this especially with my younger child. My older daughter is very close to her grandmother, but the younger — if her grandmother isn't there when she gets home from school, she says, "What's up? My grandmother: didn't she come today?" '

Faiza is a South African Muslim. She is kaumatua and manager of a Foodbank that feeds 2000-plus refugees a year. She's been here 12 years. She has three grandsons and two granddaughters. She lives with her younger sons, Jordan, 18, and Nur, 14, her daughter, and her daughter's one-year-old, Mikhail, whose father is a Maori Muslim. Faiza focuses all her grandmothering on this one child, because it is hard for her to see her other grandchildren.

'My husband came here to look for a job, and then we came, except the eldest son; he never came. He got married over there in South Africa. They visited, so we met his wife. They stayed a month. I thought they would stay here, but they went back. They have two children over there in South Africa. I have never met them. It is hard. I want to take my children from here to visit them, but they don't want to go. My son in America has one daughter. My other son on the North Shore — with his marriage breakdown it is hard to see his child. My mother had 56 grandchildren and 14 great-grandchildren when she passed away. Being part of a big family is one thing I really miss.

'The thing is, I just love to be at home with my little grandson.

My daughter is expecting another baby, due in September. She's at home, not working. As the years go by, I want to swap roles with her. I want to stay at home and look after the home, and I want her to do more study. She wants to work in HR.'

Shewaynesh's mother, Awthash, doesn't live with her. 'She lives by herself, but it is just three minutes' walk from my house. She is independent, but we see each other all the time. She nearly always comes in the morning to say "Good morning". Just to see her walking up to the window, every day, I feel my wishes have all come true. If I am not working, we might spend the whole day together at her house or at my house. She is studying English, or she was, but the government has stopped the courses for now. She is also doing sewing training. She is always busy.

'She speaks our native tongue with me and the grandchildren. It is hard for her to understand or speak English. I have a rule: the girls aren't allowed to speak English inside the house. They speak both languages well. This means that when my mother came here it was easy for her to communicate with the grandchildren, because they could understand her. The grandmother has an important role maintaining the Ethiopian language.'

Faiza: 'I speak my Afrikaans language to the children sometimes, but in the house we all speak English. My grandson has just started talking. My youngest son is called Nur, and the baby is trying to say that but he's not getting it right. You know this is the time the uncles and grandparents get nicknames — because the little ones can't pronounce their names properly.

'South Africa is like New Zealand; it's not a Muslim country. It's multicultural there, the same way it is here. I was lonely when I got here, but it wasn't too strange. I miss the mosque and the call to prayer, how you would hear it when you walked along the road, and everywhere where we lived. But I got used to that. And the services are the same in the mosque here. They are the same all over the world, always in Arabic. They will translate the Arabic into whatever language the people understand. Here, they often translate it into Urdu, because there are many Fijian Muslims here.'

Shewaynesh: 'Everything is different in Ethiopia. Grandmothers there always look after the children. And wives stay at home, so mothers and grandmothers are closer and they are all involved in child-raising. The children always love their grandmothers more than they do their mothers. In New Zealand, there are limited years that you have with your grandparents. The children stay home maybe until they are three, then it is childcare, then school. In Ethiopia, not all children get educated, because you have to be able to afford it. They don't get the education in Africa so much, but they get the love. The children are based at home, and they go outside more to play. The grandparents share their cultures with the grandchildren. Here, it is the opposite: the grandchildren need to share *their* new cultures with their grandparents! That is different.

'My older daughter graduated as a social worker. My younger daughter is doing well at school. When she has a good result, I always reward her. Sometimes I say: "You have done well, but I know you can do better than this. Do it." And then I will give her a gift. The grandchildren will be different from us. They will have a good future and happy life.'

Faiza: 'For me, it is so amazing to live with my grandson and see him growing up. I experienced seeing him being born! I help out a lot with the little one, and so do his uncles, my sons. It's the best feeling — to be a grandmother. The baby wants kisses from me. When I come into the house he just calls, "Ma, Ma!" He is so excited.'

Shewaynesh: 'My mother is a quiet person, not a talker. But the girls have a different connection with my mother, different from the way they are with me. She can help to tell them about their past. They feel the great love from her. When they are sick, they need my mother, not me. They say, "I'm sick, so can you call my doctor please." They call her "doctor" when they are sick. She heals their sicknesses. I don't know what it is that she does — I think it is maybe just touching — but you feel better.'

Faiza agrees. This makes her separation from her other grandchildren extra sad. You can't experience healing touch over Skype. 'I'm still using remedies that my mother taught me. When you have a cough or fever, I am into my ginger and honey. If my children have the flu, I don't go for doctors' medications. And castor oil is good, too. I use that for their noses when they are very little, for blocked noses. Or if they get an injection and they are crying, and the arm is swollen, castor oil will take the pain away. I learnt that from my mother.'

Shewaynesh: 'I also have traditional remedies. I use garlic and blackseed — either the oil or the seeds, or both, and I mix them with honey and mint then grind it. I take it every morning. My mother learnt this from me! I taught her! She used to have nose problems and now it is cured. So there *are* some things you can teach a grandmother!'

Faiza agreed that blackseed was good for you. I had to admit I'd never heard of it. 'It's good for allergies, too. Blackseed is in our Koran. It is one of the medications that our prophet used to use. It is good for everything. Get it from Indian or Somali shops.'

They both also agreed that children love their grandmothers more than they do their mothers.

Faiza: 'Children do love their grandmother more than their mother. Definitely. It happened with my sister's children because my parents raised them. With my children it was unusual that I raised them myself, but every weekend we went to my mother's. Me and my sisters, we spent a lot of time with our mother, sharing childcare.'

Shewaynesh: 'The grandmothers spoil the children. The parents want to show them what is good and what is bad, but the grandmothers don't care. They spoil them. Mothers say "No". Grandmothers say "Yes". When my mother is around, my daughter knows I can't growl at her, because her grandmother will defend her. Grandchildren go to grandparents to get money. They think grandparents have all the money in the world. "If you don't give to the child he will be upset with you his whole life. So give them what they want. Never keep it for yourself." That is a saying from home. The love is so strong in your heart. Children know it.'

> 'Children think grandparents have all the money in the world.'

The two women talked about the food they feed their families. Shewaynesh said her mother's cabbage dish was a family favourite, and chicken with a spicy sauce. 'I love everything she cooks.'

Faiza told me that Shewaynesh's Ethiopian coffee was popular at work, and her

Faiza Hanslo

delicious bread. 'My other son, Jordan, he loves it when I make doughnuts. He wants me to make him breakfast. "You have to have your cereal first, and then you can have a doughnut," I say. You see: I am his mother and not his grandmother!'

I asked if there can be a conflict between the way daughters live now and the way grandmothers would like them to live. Shewaynesh said it has been difficult for Awthash.

'When she first arrived, six years ago, it was hard. "They should do what the mother says," she told me. She cried about it. She said, "You are the mother. They must obey you." I had to explain that here it is different. You have to have a communication with the child. You must listen to them. That was too difficult for my mother. "The children here talk loudly with their mothers," she said. I told my mother not to worry about it. I said to her, "You feel they are talking too loudly, but it's not. I know." Now she is better. I know that if there is something not right with my children, we just sit down and listen to them. It isn't about the age of the child; it's about the communication. I'm not saying they have to do things my way. I used to be like that, but I've changed. Now my mother is used to it, but her way of coping is to keep quiet and not say anything.'

Faiza: 'It's just the new generation growing up. They have a different way of talking to you, whether you come from Ethiopia or South Africa or wherever. My son's son is on the North Shore, but I don't see them at the moment. I used to. I want them to fix things so we can see the little one again. He's six. We haven't had any experience of his going to school. It isn't nice not seeing him. He hasn't met his cousin. We do send messages, asking the mother if we can see him, but she doesn't reply and we don't know what to do about it. She is also a South African, but she is a Christian girl. My son takes him to the mosque, and she takes him to the church. They argue. Her mother and sisters moved to Australia, so the little boy has no family around him. I feel sorry for the child.'

None of the women have husbands. Faiza's former husband is in New Zealand, but doesn't ask about his grandchildren. 'I never used to say anything back when he shouted. Coming to New Zealand changed me so much. I learnt to stand up for myself and for my family, especially my grandchildren. My daughter's marriage has problems, too. Mikhail's father wanted to see the baby, and she didn't want him to see the baby. She told him he was never there for her and never gives them words of comfort.'

Shewaynesh told how the father of her first daughter passed away. 'My second daughter's father is in Wellington. Sometimes life is too complicated. I try to focus not on the bad things. I think, first, support your child and your grandchildren. I believe things happen in your life for a reason; to teach you, or to change your life. I'm not upset anymore. He has another wife. I try my best to keep a communication between my daughter and my ex-husband. My daughter said we won't speak to him until she is 18 years old.'

And their wishes for the future?

Shewaynesh: 'In the future I want to be surrounded by my grandchildren.'

Faiza does, too, but it is hard when families are shattered and scattered all over the world.

Annie Ruth

'I can't stop smiling'

'I learn from Harrison, my two-year-old grandson. It's a misconception that a child has an undeveloped brain. Rather, they have the most flexible brains, capable of learning massive amounts. So, we must learn from them.

'When I went out to Peka Peka to look after Harrison on Tuesday, I had in my bag the script of the latest play I'm directing, *Mother Courage*. I gave Harrison a page of the script to draw on. That scribble of his! All curves and angles. When I went back to directing the following day, I gave the page to the guy who plays the priest, and Harrison's scribble has become the movement pattern he has to dance when he sings his song. I think I will credit Harrison with choreography in the programme!

'There's another role in *Mother Courage* of a daughter who is dumb, unable to speak, because of some long-ago trauma. Harrison can't talk yet, so I watch, and learn how he communicates, with us and with himself. He sings to himself a lot, so I've now got the woman who is playing Kattrin to sing, to burble, to herself, like he does. I want her to play the role as a happy person to whom bad things have happened. That is more endearing, more courageous than playing a closed, sad person. We will love her for her courage rather than feel sorry for her.

'Someone else in the play has to be drumming. I watched Harrison drumming on an outside chair that had rainwater in the scoop of the seat. His delight in the splash of the water was intense. His face filled with delight and rapture. I want that actor to achieve that intense sensual delight that Harrison shows me every day I'm with him.

'I couldn't have planned these instructions to the actors. It's random. I now see Harrison as my ideal resource. He energises me in my work. When directors say "be more childlike", I find that a useless instruction. If we watch children, actual children, they can be our perfect models, because they live in the moment, without self-consciousness.

'At home I watched my partner, Jo, on the mat, playing with Harrison and sharing a moment of delight when a fire engine went past, far below. They knew their delight was shared by the other. It's that mutual pleasure in communication that I want in my theatre experiences.

'I didn't realise, before I became a grandmother, how much I'd be able to surrender to Harrison's relationship with Time, and how enriching that would be for me, too. I surrender to his time when I'm with him. I learn to be in the moment. Anne Bogart, an American theatre director, and a mentor of mine, points out that in Greek there are two words for "time": *Chronos*, clock time; and *Kairos*, time that is outside time. If you take care of *Chronos*, you make room for *Kairos*, she says. I now insist my actors arrive promptly for rehearsals. I lock them out if they are late. They've learnt to all arrive on time. That means we start immediately. We have time then for *Kairos*.

'Our family routine is this: every Tuesday I am at my son's place, an hour's drive away, by 7.30am. It frees Lisa, my daughter-in-law, to go to work. Initially, she used to work from home, then I realised that was because I didn't get there until nine, and that was too late for her. She commutes to Palmerston North from Peka Peka. So I said my commitment is that I will be there at 7.30am every Tuesday. "You can rely on that," I said. Lisa doesn't have the long swathe of time with Harrison that I have. She has the weekends, but she has to cram into them all of those other things — shopping, cooking, etc. Alex, my son, looks after Harrison on Mondays, I do Tuesdays, then he's in crèche for the rest of the working week.

'I leave here before 6.30, get a coffee on the way. On the drive, I plan things Harrison and I will do that day. I don't timetable activities. I aim for uninterrupted play. Kids are interrupted all the time by adults who want to feed them, wipe their nose — it's time for this, that, whatever — and that's shitty for the kid. I try to not interrupt him. I might wipe his nose, but we just carry on doing what he's doing. That's so different from how I was when my son was little. I didn't give poor Alex that much focus; I was so busy. But with Harrison, it's only one day a week. I can do that, intensely. That day is timeless and stressless.

'Whatever I say to him, he repeats it. He doesn't always retain it, but he is experimenting with the sounds. We went down to the sea, swings and slides. I was going "Look at the sea", and he goes "Seeeeea". We get near the waves. The water's around our feet and he's trying to get into the sea, waving his arms. He loves water. We laugh a hell of a lot together. He throws his arms around me and hugs me.

'Back from the beach, I sing to him a lot, often in Greek. I'm the flag-waver for his Greek side. I taught myself a couple of Greek lullabies, and another one about a rabbit — there are rabbits everywhere where they live. Harrison likes them. I want him to have a sense of the sound of that language. In the songs is embedded the culture.

'I've longed for grandmotherhood for so long, but I am surprised by just how delighted I am with him. I am not bored with him at all. I sit on the floor, and he will sit on my face, crawl all over me. It's hilariously funny, he thinks, to sit on me and fall backwards. All of that delights me. I don't know how long his delight in this will last, so I treasure it, because I know everything about childhood is fleeting. He won't be like that always.

'Harrison is adept technologically. He can relate through the iPad screen. I say, "Shall we call Jo Jo?", and he says, "Yessss." I FaceTime Jo from Peka Peka, and he will immediately rush to give her a kiss on the screen, and then he waves goodbye. I'm sure all kids are like that now.

'At the end of our shared day, I give him his bath and maybe a bottle. After I've put him to bed, I sing him his songs and read him his story. I keep him up a little longer so that Lisa sees him at the end of her day, then, when he's asleep, I drive home in the dark. I pull over a little way from their house and ring Jo and say I'm on my way.

'Most of the time on the drive home I think about things that have happened. I smile. I can't help it. I can't stop smiling, even though I'm in the car alone. I put my Greek language tapes on and practise speaking Greek. I practise the Greek songs I am planning to teach Harrison. Greek songs are complicated vocabulary and hard to learn. Alex likes my trying to teach Harrison Greek.

'When I'm not with him I don't mean to think about him, but he's always there. He's just in my mind. I will look at something, like a light, and I hear him saying "liiiight" and I smile. I see the world through him. Jo and I now copy his vowels. It's very attractive.

'I know he adores me. I'm "Yia Yia" (Greek for "Grandma"). Jo is "Jo Jo". They drove in on Sunday last weekend, and all the way from Plimmerton he's going "Yia Yia, Jo Jo". He runs to Jo with his arms wide open when he arrives here. He enjoys being with her, and he loves our apartment. She takes him downstairs to the gym and the pool and the spa. It's hard to have a coffee in peace when he's here — and I like a coffee in peace — but I can go and have one and leave him in the apartment with Jo.

'He loves our environment here, being so different from his rural one near Peka Peka. He loves sitting by the apartment's floor-to-ceiling windows and looking at all the cars on the Wellington streets way below. He's fascinated with all the outside lights he can see from here. He turns inside lights on and off, especially the lamp in the spare bedroom. I have this plan that we have to have him overnight for the next Lux festival. I've already told his parents. We've had him three overnights so far. The cot is next to the bed. When he wakes, he peers out and pulls at the blind. He gestures to us to pull it up. He yells "Boat! Car!" I will be negotiating for overnights to be regular features next year.

'I wish his parents would take the opportunity to go out on the town when he stays here overnight, but they are just too busy, too tired. They go to bed early when we have him. Lisa was going to Dunedin for work last week, so she dropped him off here at 6am on her way to the airport and picked him up the next night. Another time, Alex dropped him off on his way to work, then I drove Harrison home the following day. I was terrified of driving in the car with him at first. But needs must. I'm used to it now.

'He knows the waterfront, because we take him there. He chases the ducks. You look at things differently because he does. Lots of things I wouldn't notice, but I do notice now because he does, like diggers. I love the way he chews those vowels. "Dig AH." We are now on the alert for diggers.

'And I knit for him — he must have at least 20 garments I've knitted. I've just knitted some jackets for his birthday, and a Goth doll with big black boots, embroidered face, white hair. Here's one with little metal car buttons. He'll go "Caaar, caaar", because that's one of his words. Here's a cardigan with teddy-bear attached, so he can carry it around in his pocket. Beautiful colours; all my knitting is very bright. This jacket is beautiful wool. I did a Frankenstein zombie thing, with stitches in her neck. These are just the latest knitting. But I might have to slow down. My hands are finding the knitting a bit difficult now.

'When he's older, my fantasy — and I'm not taking into account how much older I am going to be — when he has problems at home as every teenager will have, I'd like to think we are the first place he will run away to. I also think they live in the country and we live in the city, the middle of the city. How boring is the country for a teenager! It will be fantastic for him to stay with us when he's a teen.

'My mum's dad was a fabulous grandfather. He was born to be a grandfather. I need to use him as my model for Harrison. When I was

'We are a bit raucous. I don't care about other people hearing us.'

little, I remember saving up for a walkie-talkie doll. He told me I could have any coins I found lying around the house. One day I went there, and there was a coin trail. Pop Pop (that's what I called him) had made a trail from the front door, up the stairs, over the bed. He'd gone to that trouble for me. He made magic in my life. He'd been a magician and a professional juggler. He left me $50 when he died, to start my acting career. Maybe I was 13. He saw that in me then. I would want to be that sort of grandparent, understanding my grandchild. Grandma showed her adoration in the food she made. She was very warm, but Pop Pop made magic.

'I give Harrison different things from what his parents give him. I am way more playful with Harrison than his parents are. I am naughty. I don't say "No"; not as his parents do. We are a bit raucous. His parents are way more restrained. We like making crazy sounds. I don't care about other people hearing us. Alex said, "I love seeing you two together", but he gets mortified in public. He's always found me a bit much. When he was bad on the street when he was a kid, I'd say to him, "You keep doing that and I will sing." It always worked!

'Both Alex and I have found what we love to do, me theatre and Alex flying, and we both are doing it, living it. I wish that every child can grow up to live their dream.'

♡

Charles and Helen Nicholls

Grandfather of the school

'I do a few things around the school,' said Charles Nicholls, underplaying his role. 'I get greeted by kids at Countdown. I hear the parents say, "Who's that you're saying hello to?" and the child says, "Arlo's grandad." Arlo is in Year 2.'

Charles does the usual things: he goes on school expeditions, and is a member of the Friends of the School fundraising group. The school has changed its decile rating. It used to be lower, and when the decile rating changed they lost $60,000.

Charles calls himself retired. He is a Justice of the Peace and volunteers for St Vincent de Paul doing budget advice. In this role he sees many grandparents who are looking after their grandchildren with very little money. Helen works full-time, a secondary teacher in Mangere. Together they look after the children in the school holidays, often with the third grandchild, Enda, who is six months younger than Lyla. Enda lives further away, near Piha.

'When it is holiday time we try to do edu-tainment. Arlo resists our doing anything that resembles teaching. I was trying to suggest to him a better way to lay out his maths calculations. He had the answers right, but they were in the wrong place. When I intervened, he said, "I don't need to do this." I thought, "It's not worth a battle." '

Helen: 'We sing a lot of folk songs from our youth: Arlo and Woody Guthrie and Pete Seeger. Lyla and Enda dance to The Beatles. We play quizzes, dominoes, board games. We go to the beach with them, or swimming pools, parks, playgrounds. We read lots of books. Charles is an ex-fencer, so he can keep up with light sabres. We aren't precious grandparents. If someone does draw on the walls — Lyla was especially creative with a ballpoint pen recently — we'll fix it. We get science experiments from library books. We made a volcano that really oozed, and exploded. My parents did this with us. They were exemplary parents.'

Charles: 'We do lots of chasing, and Hide and Seek. We do madcap things with bats and balls around the house. I find Minecraft difficult to get my head around, and Arlo is obsessed with it, but someone else can indulge that obsession for him. Our house is Party Central for the kids' birthdays. Last year, Helen bought a ninja costume for a birthday. Helen's family has always been huge birthday celebrators.'

Helen: 'I love having them here. I feel so lucky, because we are fit and well and can do this. We feel privileged, because so many of our friends have grandchildren overseas. They can't cuddle them and dance with them.'

Good parenting seems to be a tradition in this family. Charles: 'We think family history is important, and we talk to the kids about our histories. Helen's father is still alive and has 18 great-grandchildren. He's called "Gee Gee" when he's up here in Auckland. He's an endless supply of knowledge. My father — the one with the sword — moved into our back flat after his wife died, and he turned into a committed great-grandad. He stopped smoking overnight. He had the children to himself for an hour or so after school before either of us got home.'

Helen: 'I was brought up with Playcentre. My mum was Playcentre-trained. I was a Playcentre parent. I learnt all those techniques like, "Would you like to put your pyjamas under your pillow or in the drawer?" as a way of getting them to tidy up. Occasionally they outwit me, but usually it works.'

Charles: 'I was involved with the grandchildren from birth. As I was retired, I was the one in the family in a position to be useful. That early involvement has had a lot to do with my relationships with the children.'

Arlo was born in Adelaide, and Charles was there within 36 hours. 'Lizzie broke her coccyx when he was born. When he was one day old I carried him around, soothing him, while she, poor thing, had physio.' The same thing was expected to happen with her second baby, so Charles flew across and looked after Arlo and spent two and a half months in Adelaide so Lizzie could have the total bed rest that was prescribed.

While grandparenting is a major part of their lives, the Nicholls say it is important, too, to have a life of their own. 'We've been saving money, and we are going off to do our OE soon. Neither of our daughters wanted us to put off travel. We might be too old by the time the grandchildren are independent. Our girls are encouraging us to go. The kids will go into YWCA programmes, like OSCAR [Out of School Care and Recreation]. It's good socialisation. In fact, Arlo has already started some after-school activities.'

How do you think the grandchildren see you?

Charles: 'Oh, as a source of fun.'

We grandparents are necessary to society. We have skills we can still use. We are able to contribute.'

Di and John Conway

~◦∞◦~

A safe house

Di: 'When I was a young nurse, in the 1960s, I was in a surf club and friendly with John, who ran a surf shop. One day I told him I was pregnant, not to him, and he said, "Marry me and we can share the baby." But I didn't. I gave the baby up for adoption — that's what you did then. There were no child benefits. And I went to England. But I came back after a while, and I married John. The idea was to have lots of kids. I wanted babies. But that didn't happen, so we adopted our two girls.

'Twenty years later, the baby I gave up for adoption turned up. Jan. She was 21. When she walked into the family, she was another Turnbull, such a family likeness. It was so fabulous. Her adopted family embraced us. She's 50 now. I was around for the births of her children, Ashley and Brodie. I haven't been a hands-on grandma for those children because she and they live in Christchurch, but also, of course, because they have two sets of grandparents already!'

John: 'And we're going to Ashley's wedding soon. When Brodie was a kid, he said one day, "Poppa John, you are pretty good with machinery and you make all these things." And I said, "Your dad is a pretty handy man, too, Brodie." "I think I might want to do this," he said. And he is now an engineer with a formal apprenticeship in Christchurch. I like talking to him about it, and not only that: he's a bloody good rugby player. I always get a thrill out of that. I played semi-professional in England before coming out here way back when I was 19. I'm 83 now.'

Di: 'Sarah, the elder of our two adopted children, went haywire at puberty. She had drug and alcohol problems. She had a baby girl, then separated from the father. We supported whoever of them had Olivia, the baby. Sarah went away for a while. Sonny, the father, got a house up the road, and we were very involved with the welfare of both Olivia and Sonny. He dropped her off before 7.30 each morning, because he would be going to work. I'd look after her or take her to kindy, then give them both an evening meal.

'I have this craft room off the bedroom, and I said, "Right, let's make this into a bedroom for her." The idea was she went home for the weekends, but she never went home. Not for one weekend. We all just drifted into it. If we went away, Sonny shifted in here. Olivia was with us for seven years. She was brilliant at school, and became a hockey rep. She had to be dropped off early somewhere for practices. I didn't moan about it, but when it stopped I was so relieved. It freed me up.'

John: 'Olivia was a very good hockey player. If she'd carried on, she would have represented New Zealand. I took her every Friday night to the hockey stadium. It was a great thrill when I heard a college team say, "Get that number 7!"'

Di: 'I went to Social Welfare for help, as we were struggling financially. They said that because I was a grandmother I wasn't eligible

for any help. If I was an aunty, there would have been help. The law has changed now, thank goodness.

'Daughter Sarah came back, just came through the door, when Olivia was four. That was a shock. I hadn't seen her for all those years. She said she was pregnant and needed help. She was homeless, sleeping on couches, drifting. She still had a lot of issues, but she is totally my and John's daughter. We tried to help her get her life together and stop drinking. I am pro-life, but this is one case when I thought an adoptive mother would be good.

'She got her life together, she stopped drinking. I was at the birth. She chose a couple for adopting. When the boy was born, he was the first baby to be born and offered for adoption that year in Wellington.

And it was July. That's how precious a child for adoption was then. She called him Jonathan Lewis after her father.

'Social Welfare had changed their stance with adoption since I'd had had my baby adopted out all that long time ago. They now believed that, no matter what situation a mother is in, the baby is better with the mother. I don't believe that. The father had hit Sarah in the stomach when she was pregnant. It was harrowing stuff. I thought that I had to be in the front row with this adoption. I wanted that baby to be adopted by a loving couple, like Jan had been.

'Social Welfare were emotionally blackmailing Sarah to keep the baby by making it very hard to organise an adoption. The woman Social Welfare had employed to look after the baby before the adoption took place hadn't got anything ready. When we took the baby around there, she had no bassinet, no milk! Thankfully, Sarah chose a lovely couple to adopt Jonathan. He is now 6 feet 4 and he's in his final year at school. I am so grateful that they took him and gave him a happy family life.

'When children turn up, I feel compelled to help them.'

'At Christmas we get together with the adopting family. They are now part of our extended family. When Jonathan was a toddler, they turned up at one of my art exhibitions. This little toddler ran across and said "Di!" Sarah did the right thing, letting him go to a good home. I knew he was safe now. Sarah now is fine. She has her own place. In 2008, when Olivia was in the Fourth Form, Olivia drifted to her mother's place for 10 days and never came back here to live.

'Then our second daughter, Anna, came to me and said, "Mum, I'm falling in love with an older man who has a child already." His child's birth mother couldn't cope, and she handed her child to the father (who is now Anna's husband), so Anna became an instant mother. That child, River, is now totally part of our family, one of the grandchildren. I can remember him just when the law changed and you weren't allowed to smack kids. He was being an annoying little toad and I said, "I'll

'Grandads have all got stories.'

smack you, and I'll go to prison", and he burst out with, "No. Don't go there. You're good at being a grandparent!" I burst out laughing. He laughed, too, and we sat down to afternoon tea.

'Anna and her husband have three more children now. I am very involved with them, because the parents both work full-time. We have looked after those children daily for years. I get there at 8.30 and get the kids to school and kindy for morning, and have them after school.'

John: 'We were totally tied up with Anna's kids, because the parents were working so hard. We were essential. Anna forgets this now, but that's okay. River's father has a demanding job. River was good at soccer, like his dad, and I'd take him to different games all over the place while Di looked after the babies. When River went to college, he changed to basketball. One minute he was 5 feet, and then — boom — he was 6 feet, so basketball it was. I went to all of his games on a Thursday night.'

Di: 'So that is eight grandchildren overall, and there's also Jonathan's sister who is also now part of the family. We used to do a family dinner every week, like a glorified Christmas dinner — roast, with all the trimmings. Good slow cooking, all served properly, with serviettes and table manners. Everyone had a chance to talk. It was brilliant. But now the kids have so many commitments, like soccer, which means the dinner is only once a month. But the family can breeze in anytime, use the computer, just hang out. There's no instant food in the dining room, but there are always apples and bananas. The kids know to just come and help themselves.

'All the grandchildren get on. The family dinners are now turning into parties, because the grandkids are turning into young adults. At the last family dinner, Olivia, who is now 21, was with two of her cousins, and they got into the dress-up box and got out Anna's ball gowns, which my own mother had made for her, and they put them on. (I couldn't find the washing after that, and realised it had all been bundled in with the fancy dress when they tidied away.)

'In a house like this, filled with family history, there are lots of opportunities for the kids to wander around and see their heritage. This place is their ribcage, their memory house. They have stable houses where they live, but this is the history. Jackson, one of Anna's sons, got a fairy thing from the dentist, and he brought it around and asked me to look after it because "Mum would just chuck it out". Then there's the apple stickers I keep — to raise money for a soccer ball. I keep the certificates for asking a good question at school, that sort of thing. Daughter Anna has a posh house with everything in the right place, so those memory things have to find a place here.'

John: 'I tell them about the Second World War, and help with school projects. Olivia once went to the Holocaust Museum and wanted to talk to me about it. I'm Jewish. I told her a bit about the Jewish enclave in Stepney, and what happened to the family next-door. I don't think the grandchildren need to know too much about that. There are loads of books here for them to read to find out what happened, if and when they want it. They'll be more interested when they are older.'

Di: 'I am slowing right down now. I've done my bit. I'm loving not being tied into a timetable any more. John and I have our sheds back, our sheds that he built for us, for our woodwork and sculpture projects. Turning 70 gives me permission to say "No". Looking back, I see it's been dramatic, but I wouldn't change any of it. My own family, my siblings, gave me strength through all this. They were always just there. They never told me what to do. This is what a good family life does for you: it gives you strength. That is what I am trying to instil here.

'The kids are all getting on fine. I'm proud I've been responsible for giving them the chance of a good life. Throughout it all, we had to keep this house as the happy, safe house. John and I don't yell at each other. Everyone knows: this is the safe house.'

John: 'The kids have to make their own way in life. They'll turn up if they need something. I hope they all have a life as good as mine has been. I couldn't wish for anything more for them.'

Di: 'We will tidy the place up one day; the toy box can almost go. But there may well be great-grandchildren anytime soon. After all, Ashley is marrying this man in Christchurch ...'

Graham McClintock

❦

A chip off the old block

Graham McClintock has lived on his rugged hill-country farm near Cheviot for 38 years. His first love is horses. Around the walls of the farm kitchen hang ribbons won for show-jumping, and there are bags more stowed away. He still rides in the Brackenridge Hunt. But now that he is 82 years old, and with sons not interested in farming, he has a problem. Or he *did* have a problem — until his granddaughters Lulu and Georgia grew up. They turned out to be chips off the old block.

As Graham says, 'You just can't tell how a child will turn out. It's a bit like horses. I have five children, four boys and a girl. My eldest son,

Tim, is a commercial airline pilot. He's not interested in farming. All he wanted to do when he was little was drive these model planes around. He wanted to be a topdressing pilot and I talked him out of that. Too dangerous. Too many takeoffs and landings. I paid for him to get his commercial licence. $40,000 it cost. He started off by flying ski-planes.

'My son Jeff has got three girls. I gave him a farm, and the three girls grew up on it. The eldest girl was the one I thought would be into farming. She came to the Blenheim Show with me when she was 10, and she kept coming with me to dog trials. She talked to all of the dog trials people, and she finished up with a heading pup off one guy there. I thought she'd be right into farming, but then she went away to town and got interested in shoes and shoe shops, and so you can never tell. She's managing a shoe shop in Brisbane. The middle sister, Georgia, she's at Canterbury Uni of all things. She's learning marine biology! She comes to help me in her holidays. She's grabbed one of my best horses and she says it's hers now.

'Lulu, the youngest, is the farmer now. She's been working with me for the past 12 months. She spent a reasonable amount of time with us when she was little. She loved being with Jean, my late wife. When she came back to the farm after school, she was into animals, into ponies especially. She left school early — it wasn't for her — and she wanted a job. Lulu's seen a lot of different examples of ways of making a living in the family, but she chose farming. So I said to her: "You can work for me. I'll teach you." She couldn't learn that from her dad. He's a helicopter pilot, and he works month-on and month-off in Papua New Guinea. He flew for Helicopter NZ for years at Fox Glacier and Twizel. He's done five trips to Antarctica, been there for three months. That didn't appeal to her.

'In the end I expected her to come to the farm. I've got two nice horses, you see, and I wanted someone to ride them. I could see she wanted to get back into riding. She lives in the cottage down the road now, and she does everything on the farm with me. I'm less strong now, so she's a great help. She's the capable one. I teach her how to make a profit. She's got a good head on her shoulders about money. She can do mustering; sheep work, cattle work. And fencing. It's 1500 feet above sea level at the back of the farm, and the farm is 849 hectares.

It's Corriedale sheep and cattle. The mustering is best on horseback. It can be five or six hours' work. If you're on a motorbike, it's hard. Sitting on a horse you can watch the sheep and the dogs. The horse will watch where he's going. He's not going to step in a hole or hit a rock, which can happen on a motorbike.

'She was away mustering, five miles away at the back of the farm, last Sunday when I broke some ribs. Easy to do. I went to shift some hoggets, a dozen of them, in long grass. I had to cross a culvert where I cut the bailage from. I'd lost a lamb. I couldn't find him. I went back the next day and found him in the neighbour's. I only had the heading dog with me. I got the lamb in the corner, grabbed him by the back leg, and I tripped over and landed on a stump in the long grass, on my back. I kept hold of him, though.

'I have a heap of horses. I've always loved show-jumping. Lulu and me, and sometimes Georgia, we travel to Blenheim, Waimate, Christchurch to show-jumping events. I was reasonably good at show-jumping earlier on. I was in the South Island show-jumping team in 1956. Up until 12 months ago, neither of these granddaughters had done anything but pony jumping, but they are starting to come right. Lulu's not as good as I am yet, but she's keen enough to improve. When we go show-jumping, we have to arrange for someone else to be here looking after the animals. If I had enough money I would be show-jumping all the time. The grandgirls learnt how to do it by jumping on their ponies. They didn't have special teaching. I think the best way to learn is by watching show-jumping on TV, watching other riders. When we are at a show-jumping event, I get them to watch the top riders. That's the best way.

'I'm not frightened to tell Lulu off. A month ago we were show-jumping somewhere, and she wasn't doing what I wanted her to do and I just said to her, "You better toe the line." I'd spent 700 or 800 dollars on entry fees. That's without the fuel to get us to these things. I just said to her, "You have to dedicate yourself to it or I'll sell the horses." She wasn't pleased about that. The next day she told me, "I cried all night." I said, "Well, you've got to be realistic. I'm not paying this money if you aren't dedicated." I think that's fair enough. I tell her there is no use being half-hearted about something. Show-jumping isn't cheap. You have to buy the feed for the horses. They have to be fed right. They have to be shod every six weeks. That's at least $120 a horse. It can be $180 for show-jumping studs. "You've got to realise you are lucky to have someone paying the bills, because you couldn't do it yourself." That's what I said, just the once.

'You just can't tell how a child will turn out. It's a bit like horses.'

'Down near the cottage, I've got two jumpers — one for each of the sisters. Lulu was going to ride both of them, but Georgia, who is older than her, said she was having one of them. That was the one Jeff went hunting on, and he reckoned it was a good jumper. I've only ridden it once. I bought it last year because Lulu said it was a nice horse. We were up at Horse of the Year. She kept saying, "Grandad, you should buy it." I said, "I've got 30-odd horses running round the farm. I don't want any more", but she kept saying, "It's a nice horse." On the last day of the show, she said, "You better come and look at it again." So I finished up buying it, and it's called Felix. The other one is Tessa, which she's now riding. Tessa is a mare; Felix, a gelding. I would have picked Felix for her to ride, because Tessa is a bit hot, a lot more work than the other one. But she's happy with it. She thinks it's marvellous.

'Lulu learns farming from me, but she teaches me lots, heaps, about modern young people. She has all these friends from school, and she turns up here with a different girl every week virtually, girls from Christchurch, city girls who want to try farming. They haven't got the opportunity to go on the land. Lulu gets them up here, and they come out mustering and do this and that. I pay them. One of them was here for quite a while, and she loved farming, so she applied for several jobs, but without dogs it's hard to get a job on a farm. For a town girl to get a dog and keep it somewhere, and train it — that's hard. But that girl has now got a job driving tractors in Western Australia. There's one here right now, with Lulu. Lots of them just don't get the opportunity. When Lu was boarding at Christchurch Girls' High, she wanted the school to have an agriculture course and they said no, and she said, "Well, I'm leaving." That changed their minds. I don't know if the course is still running now.

'I do have grandsons, too. There's one working for me right now, in his university holidays from Otago. He's fixing the ball-cock in the trough. He lives near Winton in Southland. His father is a dairy consultant. There's another son at Ashley; he's got a son who is training to be an electrician.

'I never argue with Lulu. If she's not doing the right thing, I just tell her. I haven't got a computer and don't want one. Lulu can do the computer work. A young fella we used to look after, he bought a computer and had a farm down the road. He said, "You should buy a computer, Grandad, and put all the farm data on it, and get all your accounts done on it." I found out later it cost him far more to do his accounts even though my farm's much bigger than his. Then I found out he spent half the day playing games on the computer. I thought, "I don't want one of those. I haven't got time to play games!"

'With farming, I do what I've always done. I don't do any modern new ways. If Lu tells me there are better ways to do something, I just say to her, "Look, Lu, I've made plenty of money doing it my way and I'm not changing." You've got to change for a reason. Look at this drought we're having at the moment. All these people jumping up and down and not knowing what to do. We've had droughts before and we'll have droughts again. It's as bad as any we've had, but it is still just a drought. You get good years and bad years.'

I looked up from Graham's kitchen table as a truck rumbled to a stop. Lulu jumped out and ran into the kitchen. She told Graham she'd got transmission oil for the tractor.

'Ben can put it in. Do you want me to put it up in the workshop, Grandad?'

'Yes, please.'

'Okay, I'll do that. Those sheep are all in First Lane at the moment.'

'They should be brought down into the other paddock.'

'Tessa's lame, so we've got icepacks on her. We're waiting to see what her leg's going to do.'

'Why's she lame?'

'I don't know. It's that same right front leg that she's got those splints in. She was lame on it yesterday, and the day before. Georgia and I have been watching it. I'm thinking that I'll ride Felix on the Saturday, and if Georgia rides him on the Sunday, I'll bring her truck home, and I'll get those sheep in, because I don't want them to eat out that paddock too quick.'

'The sheep need to be down here Monday morning.'

'Yes. Robbie first said that he couldn't draft on Monday, but I've got him coming now. He phoned me back and said, "I can get a unit-load on, and we can draft and wean them all on Monday." '

'Good. Thank you.'

'There's a fence in the Poplar paddock I'm going to go and fix up. I've got the fencing gear with me. See you, Grandad.'

And the highly organised trainee farmer jumped back in her truck. I asked Graham what he hoped for Lulu's future. 'If I had my way, she'd just go show-jumping. Not farming. But I haven't told her that!'

Isabelle Isaako

Healing a grandchild with art

At every bend of the winding country road I followed out of Taumarunui, I wondered what I'd find around the next corner. The shape of the hills was always surprising. And then I was there, in the centre of the North Island, in Benneydale, amazingly a ghost town, and I wondered what I'd find. I had been told to look for a mosaic letterbox. I found it, easily. The biggest surprise was the two women inside the neat-as-a-pin house behind the letterbox. Isabelle had just had a wood delivery, and was busy stacking the wood floor-to-ceiling in the garage. Twenty-year-old Fiona was crouched over a drawing in a lounge full of art.

Isabelle explained how she came to live here, and why.

'When Fiona, my granddaughter, was a teenager, she spent long periods in hospital. She found life challenging and wasn't coping. We thought what she needed wasn't psych drugs: she always had a bad reaction to them. She needed peace. We thought somewhere quiet could be healing. We went on a big road trip all over New Zealand to find such a place. I was looking at old deserted houses. The idea was that we'd find something that it didn't matter what we did to it, somewhere I could afford, somewhere we could make into our home. And all roads seemed to end in Benneydale. We'd never heard of it before, but we thought, "Here's this place again! Why do we come back here?" I stopped and asked someone, "Who owns that house across the road?" They said, "What are you looking for?" I said, "Just an empty house that might be for sale." The guy said, "There's one next-door to me."

'I'd gone straight past it, just a big overgrown hedge. Never noticed it. When I looked through the hedge, I knew it was the right place for us. I bought it without ever coming inside it. I just went around the back, looked over the overgrown tangle of the front garden at those hills, and I thought: "This is it. This is the peace that we need." I thought it was a healing place. Since then we've learnt that local Maniapoto regard Benneydale as a healing place. Fi is a member of Maniapoto. So in a real sense we are home here, and being healed.'

Fi's first reaction was different: 'It was a falling-down place. I thought, "What have we come to? What a shit-hole." It was! It has grown on me. Back then, teenagers are focused on their cellphones and stuff. Coming here, having no reception, made me feel isolated. But now I feel it was good to break away from all that.' She added: 'We still don't have cellphone coverage. We're getting a cell tower in a month or two.'

Isabelle used to live and work in the Hutt Valley. She has looked after Fiona since Fiona was nine months old. 'I was working in a good job, managing the Theatre Services Centre in Wellington Hospital — the sterilising, decontamination and instrument centre of the hospital. My younger son had just left home one week earlier. I had one week not having to live my life around children and their needs. I actually ate out! I did things! This was good! Then I got this child. A paediatrician at the hospital decided she couldn't let this baby go home to her mother. The doctor noticed the surname and asked if I was related to the baby. "It's my granddaughter." I had had concerns before this. The paediatrician said, "If you could just have her for a week, that would be good."

'That's hard. To know that I needed to care for this tiny baby because of my daughter's neglect. It's a fine line when you love your children and your grandchildren, and you have to step into that parenting role. One day we grandparents aren't going to be here. The relationship between the mother and the child has to continue. It needs to be nurtured. I've tried *not* to be the main carer, just the grandmother. I have other grandchildren, too. The impact on a whole whanau is significant when you take a grandchild as though you were a parent. You want to be that storybook grandmother who takes the kids to the movies and the park and buys them an ice cream, but this is a different role. You are in charge.

'It's a huge sacrifice when you take on a child at a later age. Your peer group drifts away. You haven't the privilege of being able to wind down, spend time with friends. You can't do paid work. I was a diligent worker all my life. I ran a halfway house years ago, and was a probation officer, and a landscape gardener. I was used to being independent. To have to suck it up and live on a benefit is demeaning, having to go cap in hand and ask for everything. I became a single-income woman with a child who needed me.

'Fi suffered bullying at school. She was always sensitive and uncertain. She was bright, and this made it worse. Kids sense if you are vulnerable. It was CYF's decision that she should be at her mum's at weekends, but lots of bad stuff happened at her mum's place. If her mum was having a party, Fi would be ringing and I'd go and pick her up. Sometimes her mum would unplug all the phones so Fi couldn't contact me. There was a home invasion once. Fi was hiding under the bed trying to keep other, younger, kids quiet, and they saw boots clomping past. This is traumatic stuff that builds over time, and eventually a child's mind can't take it anymore.

'Fi began to slide off the planet. She got sick. She texted me one day from school and said she didn't feel well. She was taken to the mental health unit. They never told us anything, just put her on drugs. She's been on pysch medicine since she was 14. Not a good thing. Therapy would have been better. I remember an oral presentation she did in the Seventh Form. She found out that a lot of the psych meds they give young people actually increase suicide ideation. They become more at-risk. No one prepares you for this. It has been a huge learning experience for us both. She's still fragile, but she's coming out the other end now. Your world gets small. You focus on just getting this child through. That's huge, when you are a grandparent.'

One psychiatrist told them that children with mental health issues won't achieve. Fi has proved him wrong. 'I always knew she was capable. I'd take Fi for a slow walk every night when she was little. We'd notice everything, and I'd explain things. I'd even chant off the periodic table. I'd just learnt it, because I was studying science then. Fi absorbed all this and could chant the whole periodic table. Just a kid!'

Fi's been fascinated with science since those walks. She has received two scholarships for art, a top pass in digital technology, and the Ruth Crisp Prize in English at Te Kura. An NZQA scholarship now pays for all her materials for art school. And she's won a scholarship from an art school, which pays all her fees.

She does this art study extramurally, but in July she is moving to Wellington permanently. Isabelle will support Fiona until she is settled safely in a flat and at art school. Then Isabelle will turn Fi's room in Benneydale into an art studio of her own.

I asked them how this transformation in Fiona happened.

'When Fiona first got sick, I was caring for my mum as well. Mum was dying of cancer. After she died, I went to the Learning Connection. It was part of my grieving process. Until then, I hadn't done any art. To help Fi, I gave her paper and pencils and she drew these faces. We didn't even know then that she could do it. It became the most important way for her to express herself. For a long time we had to pull her away from drawing, because it took up all her reserves, made her vulnerable.

'We needed a vehicle for change. We needed to bring Fi back. We needed a carriage to get there, to move forward. Art has been our way of moving forward, being able to deal with bad days, enjoy the peace, bring it in as well as going out to see it. We've worked to make peace a comprehensive part of who we are. I'm so proud of Fi, because she has overcome horrendous difficulties and she excels.

'We decorated the mailbox with mosaics. We have craft days. We do stuff: art makes you well. It creates pathways that uplift you. You just get lost in the process. It relieves stress. We do all these things you see around the house. We make terrariums, gardens, have collage days. I'm always on the lookout for rubbish that we can turn into art. I encourage Fi to bake. When you make things, it allows you to wake up singing. Our lives are works of art.'

I had admired the round mosaic pedestal table in the lounge, covered with Fi's art books and drawings, and the bathroom ceiling covered with hundreds of detailed painted flowers. Fiona showed me her visual diary, full of exquisite portraits. She told me how she lays a tablecloth on the floor and does her painting lying down.

'Nan is all about 3D and mosaic. I'm more into portraiture.'

'But I've given her a love of 3D. She can now sculpt a figure. As majors for art school, she's nominated drawing and 3D. Her minors are painting and design. There's a force in me that wants everything that is good for Fi.'

'I spoil you, too,' said Fi. 'Bought her a tablet. Cooked her dinner. I used to cook every second night. I tell her I love her.'

And Benneydale has helped with the recovery, too.

'The people in Benneydale have never treated Fiona any differently. They've always gone out of their way to support her. When a trucking company here found Fi was trying to do her studies, they said, "Come and use our office anytime. We will leave it open for you. You can use the photocopiers, computers, internet." A nurse here, Laurel, has been so kind. When Fi succeeded at Te Kura, a couple of local women came around and told Fi how proud they were of her. They said they'd like to pay for her to go to Wellington for the graduation ceremony. No one meddles with anyone else, but you come back from town and there will be vegetables on the doorstep or groceries. No one says, "I left that there." It just happens. That nurturing is the thing that has allowed me to put something into me, to let me put something into Fi. That's been important; if you give all the time, you get used up and you get exhausted. If I've been to rock bottom, the goodness of others uplifts me.'

And there have been rock-bottom times. Five years ago, after a mishap in hospital, Fiona had no feeling from the waist down and couldn't walk. After emergency transportation to Starship, she was discharged: they put her down the laundry chute. 'What do I do? How do I get her into the car?' Isabelle remembers asking. They got back home somehow, but had no wheelchair. Isabelle had to pull the rugs aside and drag Fi around the house. She got an old office chair and gradually trained Fiona to pull herself along. Finally they were given a wheelchair. They waited six months for a neurological assessment. The neurologist suggested Isabelle try to get Fiona standing again.

'If we went into town, it was 8 to 10 lifts of the wheelchair and her into the boot and out again. This problem made me realise that there is only us. It was getting to be too much for Fi. I remember saying to her in the car: "We have to be strong. We will get through this, Fi." And we did.

'Sometimes we have medical appointments in Hamilton, so we stay a few nights there with adored little cousins and an uncle, or we will go up there to babysit, like we will do this week. Hamilton is only one and a half hours. I don't want you to think we are isolated. Fiona has both Maori and Samoan influences in her life. Our home is everyone's home. Our family is wider than just a nuclear one. We absorb people. Fi appreciates that there are all these aunties and uncles who are interested in her life, whereas if it was just Mum and Nan that could have been too narrow. I have 11 grandchildren and three great-grandchildren. I love them all to bits. With all my grandkids, being close to them is a privilege. It allows you a glimpse into a time we will never really see. It lets us have some input into the future.

'Being close to grandchildren is a privilege. It lets us have some input into the future.'

'The time required for Fi has made my world become so small, which is a sadness. I managed to spend some time with the others, but not the time I'd like to go to their school things, to be a traditional nanny.

'I'm also sad when I think of the financial struggle this has been. Finances are hard. Travelling for Fi's medical appointments — we have travel assistance money, which is great, but you have to have six trips to one place (it could be Starship, which is a long way away) before they will reimburse you. And then they only pay you a percentage back. Then there are the unreal expectations: a psychologist told me to take Fi to Hamilton to the movies. Hello? Where's the money come from for that? I haven't been able to save for my retirement. I'm looking at a bleak retirement. But if you asked me if I'd do it again, I would.

'Fi's mother died just before Fi's twentieth birthday. It was terrible, because Fi never got the chance to develop that relationship with her mother. Just two years previously, Fi and her mother had become friends. I had been working to maintain the relationship between daughter and granddaughter, and it was happening finally, then suddenly it wasn't there anymore. A door closed that we didn't want closed.'

Fiona looked up from her visual diary. 'My nan's like my rock. She helped me through the bad times. Without her I wouldn't be here today. We hug a lot. If I get down in the dumps, I just sit with Nan. She'll massage my head and we'll talk. It helps me get through some things.'

Isabelle looked at the diary, too. 'I would say that our grandchildren *are* our treasures. When we are older, we appreciate that more. Look at these pencil drawings with the soft graphite, portraits of children done when Fi was 15. Look at the eyes. That's trust. When they put their little hands in yours, you know they are giving you their trust.'

♡

What grandparents don't like

- The colour pink.
- Modern convenience food.
- Consumerism.
- Computer breakdowns.
- Climate change.
- Catching the kids' bugs.
- Modern education.
- Grandparents' sheds used as family storage units.
- Grandchildren having too many toys.
- Kids watching screens too much, not playing outdoors.
- That moment when they say goodbye and go off with their parents without a backward glance.

Christine Jamieson

Going to London to be nanny

Christine spent all her working life in Wellington. Her first grandchild, Mischa, was born there six weeks before Christine's husband, Kevin, died. Christine and Kevin have two daughters, and both of them had settled overseas with non-New Zealand husbands. Daughter Meredith had settled in London, and daughter Erana was in France. Christine suddenly found her life had lost motivation and meaning. She was at retirement age, still working, but not particularly happy at work. Both her house and her heart felt empty.

She went over to visit, and while she was there the daughters asked: 'Why don't you come over here?' Christine told me, 'I thought about it a little when I returned home. In fact I took five months to decide to go, then I gave work three months' notice. I cleared out my house, and returned to London. I hadn't decided what I was going to do with my retirement in New Zealand, so it made sense. It seemed like I was having a break from my life.'

I interviewed Christine while she was in London.

'My daughters were both in London now, and another two grandchildren were born here. I didn't consciously think I'd be more useful over here. I just thought it'd be nice to be closer to my girls and to be near the grandchildren, to get to know them. I did think a bit about looking after them. It just seemed like the next step in life.

'I am cautious. I took one step at a time. When I came over, I didn't rent my New Zealand house out for the first six months, to keep my options open. I had a friend who house-sat for me until I decided I was going to stay for a longer period of time.

'The London family home was one house with both families living in it, four adults and three kids. There was elder daughter, Meredith, married to Michael. Mischa is now six, and Liam just three. Our younger daughter, Erana, married to Herve, was there, too, with Alexandre, who will be one next month. There was no room for me in the house. I rented a tiny flat here. I've been where I am for two years now. Both of my daughters work full-time and their husbands stay at home with the kids. Both girls have good jobs that make enough money for their families to live on.

'Erana and Herve and baby Alex have just two months ago moved into a flat of their own, not far away, so the house has a bit more room.

'I don't have regular time to see the kids. I see both sets of families once or twice a week. I offer to take the children places. I'm the exciting nanny who takes them to exciting places. That's what most nannies do. I might take Liam to a Stay and Play. London has interesting places that are family-friendly, and people here are okay about kids. Sometimes they don't like buggies on buses, but that's the only problem. A lot of

Tube stations don't have lifts, so there are always lots of stairs. You just plan it before you set out.

'I take them to cafés to eat muffins, chocolate muffins. Mischa likes cafés as much as I do. It's all part of the nanny treat thing.

'London is great for playgrounds. There are lots in walking distance or easy to get to on the bus. We don't have a car. That's a lifestyle difference. If I was in New Zealand I guess I'd put the little ones in a car and take them somewhere. We use public transport, and London has brilliant public transport, or we walk. It's all flat and there's no wind. The rain is straight down, not horizontal rain like Wellington. Even if it's raining, it's easy to walk. They do very fancy buggies here.

'For a birthday treat for Liam, I took him to the Science Museum on the bus. In the basement of the Science Museum there's a good children's play area. He played there with water. Then we had lunch. He's into cafés, too. Then we went up and looked at railway engines and space rockets. He was so interested in the old railway engines that I think I will take him to the Transport Museum at Covent Garden. At 2.30, I said I thought we should go home. I hadn't taken the buggy, so we walked along the subway to the Tube. His little legs were getting slower and

'It just seemed like the next step in life.'

slower. In the end I carried him for five minutes. He weighs a ton. We climbed down the steps to the Tube, got on the train, and he fell fast asleep. It's easier to get to the Transport Museum at Covent Garden. He won't have to walk so far.

'The children come to stay with me, not together, but separately. That's great for them, because they have my undivided attention then. They love to stay here. It's a treat. They each come once every three weeks or so. Liam's just started doing it. There's no competition for attention. My place is very small. They sleep in the same bed as me. They love that. I'll take them out somewhere, and then bring them home and cook them a meal that they like. They go to sleep in 10 minutes flat.

'They may be the main reason I'm in London, but I also do lots of other things. I have a busy social life. I've made many new friends. I go for walks, belong to a social club. Some days I stay at home and blob!

'When I went back home to New Zealand this February I realised how much I missed the people there, and the sound of the birds. I miss family in New Zealand — I have two sisters there — and my house. London is great with new things to see all the time, but I think I've reached the next stage in my life, so I've decided I'm going back at the end of this year. I haven't worked out what I'm going to do when I return home, but I am sure I will find something.

'A part of the reason I came to London was that it was a way of grieving. I needed to get away. If Kevin had been alive, I wouldn't have done it. We had been in London together about 10 years ago, which is why I felt comfortable coming over, because I had done it before, with Kevin.

'How do I feel to see my grandchildren grow up as Londoners, not Kiwis? They certainly speak with an English accent. That's odd, because my son-in-law is Canadian, so neither of those parents have English accents, but Mischa sounds very English. She plays with English children and watches English TV. They don't know anything different. Wherever Mummy and Daddy are, that's home. But there's not much difference between the way children grow up here or there. The house I live in here has a back garden for little ones to play in. They play the same way here as they would over there. It's strange to see five-year-olds in school uniforms; that's the only difference I can think of!

'As a family, we still do typical Kiwi things. We were all together for the Rugby World Cup, for that first game. Erana and Meredith and I went to Cardiff to watch the All Blacks playing Georgia. The husbands stayed home to look after the babies. That's not so typical, but then we girls are the Kiwis!

'I'll miss all the walking when I leave. In New Zealand I'll have a car, but here I walk a lot. I'll miss going to many different places. I'm always finding new places to look at here. Big cities can be easier to live in for older people than living in smaller places. I've got used to lots of other people around, and lots of facilities.'

'When you come back, what will it be like to leave the children?'

'I try not to think about that. I am really going to miss them. They will miss me, because I'm part of their group of grown-ups. They are lucky to have this group of grown-ups who they see a lot of. That will stand them in good stead. I will have to go back to London every couple of years to see them. I'll miss reading to them. When they go to bed, I always read to them, and now Mischa reads to me. They get two stories each per night. Julia Donaldson is a favourite. I think Erana and Herve and Alex will probably go back to New Zealand. The other ones, I'm not sure. But at least the children all know me now. If I go back home, they won't forget me. Even baby Alex knows me. It has been worth it.'

Ideally, grandparents should have

- Patience.
- A driver's licence.
- Skype.
- Wet wipes.
- Sticking plasters with pictures on them.
- Fast internet connection.
- A smart-phone.
- Walls full of family photos.
- Perfect pitch and a great singing voice.
- A big outside table.
- A shed.
- A walled, wild garden with a flat, mown lawn.
- Neighbours who will throw the balls back.
- An endless supply of pasta and yoghurt.
- Board games and dice.
- Deep pockets.

Diana Menefy

❧❧

There in a crisis

Diana and Keith Menefy have three children, and farm at Hikurangi in Northland. They feel lucky because all of their children and their seven grandchildren live relatively close. Nyrene, their daughter, is the furthest away, in Rotorua. Son Mike is an hour and a half up north, and Dylan has his own place, five minutes' walk away, on the family farm.

'I felt a responsibility to meld the family into a unit. I grew up very close to my cousins, and even now it is a fabulous relationship. Time matters nothing to cousins. It seemed sad that my own kids didn't grow up close to their cousins. I wanted that close kinship of cousins for my grandkids, and the way to do it would be to bring the grandchildren together in the Christmas holidays, at our place.

'When Rhys was five, Ryan four and Declan three — that's one boy from each child — we started having Grandparent Week here. I dedicated myself to them for a week of planned activities. They are all outside kids who are used to being on the land. They all had gumboots. It wasn't that I offered them totally different experiences. The magic part of it was that they were doing it together. Now that Rhys is 17, Ryan 16 and Declan 15, they are very close friends.

'Each day had one special thing. And the rest of the time was just play. We were the only family place with a river; none of their parents had a river. So we swam and built boats, and they'd sail them in the river. We went on bush walks, and played in mud holes. I'd take photos of them so they'd each go home with an album of all the things they'd done. As a grandparent, you are a connection to the past. Your children don't have an interest in the past. When they get older and have that interest, often grandparents are gone, so the history is lost. Those little wee photo albums I made for the kids about Grandparent Weeks — they will treasure them.

'Most important was frog-hunting: all of the grandchildren have loved catching frogs. We have a pond close to the house, with goldfish in it. Once Ryan wanted to collect fish eggs so he could have goldfish in his own pond. He collected all these eggs out of my pond into a jar and took them home, and they all turned out to be tadpoles!

'On the bush walks, they had to find various things, like dragonflies and spider webs. Or we'd drive out to watch whatever was happening on the farm. I taught them to make biscuits and ice cream. We did colouring in. I used to put a roll of paper down on the floor, and they'd cut out fish or something and make a big mural. I always had Lego on hand for them, and paints and an easel. They'd make model planes out of balsa wood. We'd read, too, and we had a quiet time, reading, before they went to bed.

'As they got older the holiday changed, because their interests changed. We set up a games room, a place where they could all play, regardless of the weather, downstairs in our new house. There was one in the old house, too.

'The special holidays have given all of the kids memories of barbeques and farm life. Some of them will work on the land. Rhys is hoping to get into agriculture training. Declan is already relief-milking, not because he wants to be a dairy farmer, but it's where he can earn money. It's hard for rural kids to earn money.

'When another four grandchildren came along, the younger ones didn't have the same closeness, but they still love being here. If they go catching koura with the net in the creek, Ethan, the eldest one of that group, loves being the responsible older one, because he's the younger brother in his own family. Hannah, the youngest, and the only girl, is six. She and I went frog-hunting last holidays. It's a moment of being very quiet and still and slow. It's a lesson in being patient. Hannah is a tomboy, and patience is hard for her. I say, "Now, Hannah, quiet. The frog is there. See?" and she yells, "Where?", and the frog jumps away.

'I don't do as much grandparenting now. I wasn't working when I had those first grandsons, but, now I am busy at Northtec, the younger kids come twice a year (April holidays for Byron, and the October holiday for Hannah), and of course whenever we can fit grandchildren in during the Christmas holidays. When everyone comes for Christmas, they all get on together, but there are two groups: the older ones and the younger ones. Last Christmas I had to get Hannah a pink pellet gun, because she wanted to be part of the boys' gunfight with pellet guns in the downstairs play area, which they'd turned into a fort. They wanted the older boys against the littler ones, but I made them split up. I insisted they choose equal teams.

'As a grandparent, you are a connection to the past.'

'The families have to be at home now to look after their own animals, so we don't get together so much. It's the normal process of life. You see the grandchildren most when they are young, and then it gets less frequent because they get so involved in their own lives. It becomes just phone calls and emails and Christmas. Not even every Christmas. If Mike is contracting and doing all the silage, he's running around with machines until 2 or 3am, so he doesn't want to drive after that. He just wants to blob out on Christmas Day. So I take a hamper up there for them before Christmas.

'The kids don't often go out on the farm with Keith, because it's too dangerous. But if he's on his bike shifting cattle, they love to go on their bikes, too. There aren't a lot of things they can do with him. These days it's illegal to do things that we used to do as kids, like milking. We used to hop onto the tractor tray and go off, but things are so different for the grandchildren now. It's Declan's first year in the shed. He doesn't know how to move around stock, when to step back, how to judge that. We grew up on farms and learnt that early on, because we were out with the stock all the time. Our own kids were in the shed quite often, when they were Declan's age. But these are the new Health and Safety rules.

'At our house, my own rules apply for the grandchildren. No running inside is Number One. I remember once Dylan was chasing Mike, and Mike went to push open the French doors, missed the wood, put his hand right through the glass and ripped his artery. Emergency trip to A and E. He was lucky I'm a trained nurse.

'Another rule is: No playing with fire. I saw what fire can do when I was nursing. Never go down to the river alone. Don't go swimming on your own. There always has to be an adult. Last Christmas, even though the kids were 14 and 12, I was still nervous. I said they could go, then in the end I went, too. I sat up on the bank and read a book while they swam. I used to have nightmares about them drowning. Hannah and Byron weren't allowed to stay with us on their own until they were old enough to obey me. I have to be able to trust them. I have work to do, and can't watch the two little ones all the time. There are three dams around the house. Then there's the fishpond, and the river, too. I dread deep holes. I'm not fast enough to be able to catch them if there is a problem, and they could drown so quickly.

'Now that the older ones are teenagers, there's no reading to them in bed. Now, especially when they are here and they haven't seen each other for ages, I just say, "You wake me up, you're in trouble. Keep the noise down." They know I mean it.

'Another responsibility I have taken on is to teach them all the value of money. They want to earn money, so I invent jobs for them to do to earn money. When I do a massive amount of weeding, they load the wheelbarrow and take the weeds away. The three eldest spent one Christmas holidays chipping away the rocks and making a smooth pathway around the top of one of the dams. They pruned the hedges and mowed the lawn when my knees were crook. I bought Ethan an iPod, but it's a three-way split from me and Dylan, his dad, and Ethan himself. He has to pay back his third by working for me and contracting to read at least two chapters of a book, any book, every week. He'd far rather play on Xbox. He filled four sacks of pine needles for me. I need them to be put under the strawberries and around the melons. I paid him for those. That's money off the $144 he owes me. All kids now need to learn that money isn't there just to be handed out. It is to be earnt. They also learn that they have to manage the money they earn.

'I've put in much more involvement with Declan and Ethan than for the other grandchildren, because they are right there on the farm, just a few minutes away, and also because their mother, Sarah, died of a brain tumour. While Sarah was crook, the boys helped Dylan look after her. I saw my role as a driver and general helper. Sarah taught them to be independent. She was determined not to die until the boys could cope. Dylan took time off work to care for her with the boys, and after she died he stayed off work to be with the boys for a whole year. He is still the main caregiver. I am just the support person in the background, to be there when needed. I feel my role is often the feminine part that a male doesn't see. I've been the one to listen to them. They know if anything is wrong they can phone and I will be there. For quite a while I'd be there after school with them, because they were too young to be on their own. I'd pick them up off the school bus, and I'd be the first person they'd talk to, so they'd tell me about their day. I always recognised their moods. If it was a good day, I'd ask: "What did you do at school today?" If it was a bad day: "What happened?"

'Ethan is just finishing intermediate now, and Declan is doing NCEA 1. Dylan drops the boys at the school bus site in the morning and takes off to Kerikeri, where his business is, and they wait for 20 minutes for the bus to come. In the summer they now ride their bikes down to the bus stop. At home they always make their own lunches. Even when they spend the night at our place, they get up in the morning and make their own lunch (except sometimes I spoil them and make it for them).

'Every now and again there might be a problem with one of the kids, and I'll tell Dylan before he gets home so he can handle it. They are so responsible, the kids. If I do pick them up from the bus, I park outside their place. I remind them to make sure to get the dishes done from the night before, and get the washing in. Every now and again I'll tell them to tidy their bedrooms. During the holidays, they tidy their bedrooms properly. I take them clothes shopping, but even that is changing. This Saturday Dylan is taking them shopping, for the first time in five years. They take turns making the dinner, having it ready for when Dylan comes home from work. Declan used to do a lot of the cooking, but now Ethan is older and he does it, too. I'm there as a nagging voice. Sometimes when I'm home after dropping them off, I'll phone and say, "Have you got that washing in yet?" It's me making sure everything is moving along. Sometimes, in the weekends, they will leave the housework and all go off together motocross riding. Great! You can always catch up on housework, I say, but you can't catch up on good times.

'I'll still be at their school events, and Dylan knows that he can ask us to have the kids whenever it's needed. They are part of my daily life. When they are away I miss them. They enrich my life.

'Grandad Keith is a quiet person, in the background. He plays cards with them, and took them to the Luge in Rotorua the last time I managed to get him to leave the farm. When there is something they need, he will sit down and work with them to make it happen. He's there for them in a different way. He'll set them up on the computer and show them how to work it. He doesn't do the hands-on stuff I do; that's not his role. He helped Ryan learn to ride a bike. Ryan had been here when Ethan came off his bike and broke his leg badly. Ethan was racing Declan down the track, and going way too fast. His bike hit a stick and he was thrown off into a big hole, bike and all. Declan pulled him out so he didn't drown, then he came screaming back for help. Ryan was really shocked by Ethan's accident. He got the idea that riding a bike wasn't safe, so Keith spent hours pushing him around the farm tracks, holding the bike so he could get his balance. That's the sort of thing Keith does. I couldn't do that. I'm not fit enough.

'I regret that I never picked up the dyslexia that runs in the family. It wasn't until Declan was 12 and staying with me when he had the flu, and I got him to write me a story. I took one look at his writing and clicked instantly that he was dyslexic. Byron is also dyslexic, and we've only just picked that up, too. I gave him a dragon book for Christmas, and his mum said he wouldn't be able to read it. Then I thought, "Hey, what's wrong?" I got him to read to me, and he read by making up stories from the pictures. He had been fooling Mike, his dad. Mike hadn't been watching the words on the page, just listening to the story Byron was telling him.

'Within a week I got Declan a Speld teacher. He was already starting to fail at school. His mum complained that they sent the same three books home this year as last, as readers. That wasn't helpful. Why didn't the school check Declan out? It's a small school. They should have noticed. The teacher just put it down to Declan's grief, because he withdrew into himself when his mother died. But anyone who'd seen his handwriting should have known. All his letters were back-to-front or upside-down. Dylan is dyslexic. I'm slightly dyslexic. Two of my brothers were. I can't believe I didn't pick it up earlier. Declan's now had three years of help and it's almost sorted out.

'They are all happy children, lucky children because their parents all are together. Dylan is on his own because of Sarah's death, but he will find someone else in the future. I am a great believer in "it'll happen". We always have lots of hugs with the kids. It doesn't matter how old they are, there is something about touching. It is so important.'

♡

Diane Hebley

Grandparenting at a distance

One of Diane and Gary Hebley's sons married a Swedish woman. The young couple spent a year in New Zealand when their little boy, Leo, was one. 'We did have contact with our grandson for that year, and even then, as a tiny thing, he would take us by the hand and show us his toys. Such a generous little fellow! I'm sure we formed a relationship with him then. The Swedish wife had been to New Zealand before, but she wasn't happy here, and in the end she and our Dave separated.

'The divorce has gone through. They have shared custody. For Dave to have contact with his son, he has to live in Sweden. He sees Leo five days out of 14. Dave's an airline mechanic. He works long hours, and then has time off with Leo. His very accommodating bosses make it possible for him to have that time with his son. We are grateful to the Swedish set-up for treating Dave well.

'Our contact with them now is through Skype, which enables us to keep that face-to-face contact. When he's on Skype, Leo always has something he wants to show us. He sees our response on-screen, and we see his. He's sharing what he's been doing. I'm not a techno, but Skype is so much better than phones. It is immensely valuable to us. I bless Skype.

'For a while Leo would say, "Why can't you come and see me?" That's hard to get around, because you don't want the grandchild to think you don't want to see them. We have been able to visit him two or three times in recent years. At one stage we bought him a globe, hoping that the physical ball would help to show that we live here and he lives there and that it is a long way away. We were talking to Leo one night, and we said that it was time for us to go to bed now. And he said, "The sun is shining." We said, "The moon is shining here." He said, "Can I see your moon?" We took the laptop outside and turned it around, and he could see the Taradale moon. He was fascinated by this.

'His father speaks to him in English and his mother in Swedish, so he's bilingual. When he is with English-speaking people, he becomes more and more fluent. I was over there last year when he was four, and he was chattering away like any Kiwi four-year-old. Sometimes on Skype he forgets we don't speak Swedish and he changes to Swedish, then his father helps him out. Sometimes he forgets the English word for something, too.

'He's well supported there, and enjoys going to school. For birthdays and Christmas, we either send money and get his dad to choose something appropriate for him, or we select some books and send them. We give him only New Zealand books. *Hairy Maclary* is a favourite. He has a soft-toy Hairy Maclary.

'His Swedish grandparents are very supportive. I'm glad for his

Swedish grandmother, because he is her only grandchild. We at least have three others, in Auckland. But that's also grandparenting at a distance, because they aren't here on a daily basis. So we don't have regular family weekend dinners. We don't Skype with the Auckland ones. They are older and busier. We do phone a lot, and go up quite often and stay with them. It's a very concentrated time we have, when we are with the three in Auckland.

'Our daughter, Katherine, has two daughters, and our son, Matthew, has one daughter. The three granddaughters all go to the same dance school. We go up when something is on — a concert perhaps, or when the girls are involved in something. The girls are pleased to see us. They hug us, then we settle into the household and life goes on. We help where we can. We leave Napier by 8am so we can get there in time to do whatever pick-ups and drop-offs are required. The girls are very busy with ballet and gym.

'We drank Champagne. It was a fun night. That's how I recommend you manage grandparenting.'

'We had one lovely afternoon in Auckland recently. Both Katherine and Andrew were busy, and granddaughter Emma needed new shoes, so I got the task of taking the girls shopping. We got the train to Sylvia Park, and walked around and found the right shop. That's not a regular event for me, but it was a special, happy occasion, and a useful thing to do.

'When we farewell them after an Auckland stay, we trust we will see them again shortly, so those farewells aren't emotional. When we get back here to Napier, we are tired. We get on with our busy lives, the sort of lives we couldn't do if they were here and we were more involved with their routines. But after a while I always say to Gary, "Let's go to Auckland again. Let's enjoy it while we can."

'They all call me "Grandmama", and Gary is "Grandad". I just like the lilt of the name. It has a good rhythm. The three Auckland ones don't know their Swedish cousin much, but they do Skype a bit from time to time. We are a close family. We like being all together. It does break my heart that our son Dave is in Sweden, but what can you do? You want him to do the best he can. And he is doing that. When will he and Leo be out here again? He isn't free to make that decision himself. We wait and see. It is all grandparents can do.'

How we relate to our own children as parents

- We are guests in their house.
- We don't say, 'They are never any trouble when they are with me.'
- We don't correct their manners in front of their parents.
- We don't criticise the chosen name, or its spelling.
- We try to be helpful, but never too helpful.
- Basically: never give advice unless it is asked for.
- If we hear ourselves saying, 'You should …' or 'We always used to …' or 'Why are you … ?', we stop, breathe and start again.
- The beliefs and values of grandchildren are the parents' responsibility, not ours.
- We were more permissive parents. Now routine is back in vogue; it fits in with working parents and their inflexible schedules.
- Grandchildren are not our own children. Their parents are the most important people in their lives.

Glenda Burkett

When children's marriages fail

Family trees can be less a tree trunk and more a tangle like muehlenbeckia (pohuehue) bushes. Glenda's first husband left six months before the birth of their daughter, Elaine. With her second husband, Phil, Glenda has another two children, Michael and Lauren. Elaine had three children before her own marriage broke up. 'Elaine's eldest, Lucia, who is 11, has just done a family tree for school,' Glenda told me. 'She knows that Grandad Phil isn't her "real" grandad, but I don't think it matters to her. Phil considers Elaine's three — Lucia, Harry and Flynn — to be his grandchildren as much as Oliver, Caitlin and Leo are.' Michael had a daughter, Caitlin, and son, Leo, with wife number one. He is now married to Donna, who has a girl, Kate, from a previous marriage. Donna understands complex; she herself has a step-father whom she regards as her father, just as Elaine does. Lauren married Dan, and they have Oliver, aged two and a half.

To make it even more complex, Elaine's family are in Cambridge, some distance from the tiny settlement of Manunui, south of Taumarunui, where Glenda and Phil live and work. Lauren's family lives on the Gold Coast, and Michael's family lives even further away, in Doha.

I asked Glenda what she and Phil did to help their grandchildren through the mysterious stresses of marriage break-up.

'We provided support for the grandchildren. When Michael's marriage broke up, it affected four-year-old Leo worse than it did his elder sister. She was very much Daddy's girl anyway. We knew that between the two very stressed parents, the children sometimes weren't getting the attention they needed. We tried to provide security and stability, to visit as often as we could, to have them with us in the weekends, with or without Dad, and to do things with them, all the things parents do. It is hard on kids when their parents separate. Kids don't have the perspective that an adult has.

'When Elaine's marriage ended, we supported her three children in just the same way we had supported Mike's children, trying to provide security, being there, making it clear that we loved them, that we weren't going anywhere and that we would always be there for them. Then, later, we tried to ease the transition to new houses and sometimes new relationships.

'Because Phil and I have a happy marriage, our kids all anticipated that their marriages would be, too. It was shocking for both Mike and Elaine to find that their partners had feet of clay. It was heartbreaking for me, too, to see my children upset. In both cases my children were the wronged parties, and I felt terrible for them. I saw them going through the same thing I myself had been through: a partner being unfaithful.

'Elaine was too upset to tell me this dreadful news. She sent me an email. I still have it. "All support and hugs gratefully accepted" is how the email ended. I felt particular sorrow and outrage for Elaine, because her father, my first husband, had been an absent father. He's never even seen his grandchildren. I felt she'd been abandoned and betrayed by the men in her life, except her step-father Phil, and her brother, Michael. Michael, of course, knew what she was going through.

'She went to WINZ to see what support she was entitled to for the children. Flynn, who was only three or four, heard his father screaming abuse at his mother in the street. I felt tremendous anger. It was hard not to fall apart. At the same time I knew I had to bite the bullet and be polite because of the grandkids. Phil was escorting a group of kids on a trip to Japan. We didn't tell him until he got back. He was furious.

'Michael and his ex had this shared-custody arrangement, half a week each, which wasn't ideal for the children. Elaine and her husband also have joint custody. It was a long time before I could bring myself to speak to the exes. Elaine is wary of forming a new relationship, because she doesn't want to destabilise the children again. The ex now has a new partner. The older children have accepted it, but Flynn found it hard. We always felt Flynn needed extra love.

'When the new partner moved into the ex's house, Flynn became very naughty at school. One Saturday, when the two others had gone to their soccer game, we were colouring-in together and he said, "Daddy's got a girlfriend now", and he told me a little. He didn't have any questions for me, but he needed to process in his own mind that this was really happening. When I went home I found the Hairy Maclary toy which he's always liked. I sent it to him, with a letter saying, "I'm worried about Hairy. He's been sitting in my Reading Recovery room at school and he's feeling neglected and unhappy. Do you think you could look after him?" Elaine told me that Flynn took Hairy everywhere for three weeks. I hope it helped him ease the transition and the realisation that a new woman was part of his father's life.

'Mike's new partner, Donna, has the same values we have. They met in a park, on the suggestion of friends. Mike took his kids and his dog along to the meeting. Donna saw how loving he was with them, and she liked that. We related to her immediately. Mike's kids love her now, too. But nothing is straightforward. Donna got a posting in Doha and off they all went. Caitlin is now a 13-year-old sophisticate, having many friends at the International School. She probably finds it hard to relate to her mother here.

'It is always difficult in any family when people have different values. We don't value huge cars, the latest gadgets, etc. We value how well you live your life and how good you are in life. We want to consciously model that for our grandchildren. I just hope the grandchildren will see the way we live our lives and recognise our values as being ones they respect.

'The grandchildren have never asked us questions about all these family relationships. I think it will come, in time. I've always been prepared to answer them, but you can't sit down and say to them: "Tell me how you feel." I am more than willing to talk to them if and when they do ask questions; honestly and, I hope, without too much prejudice. But I do still find my teeth gritted when I have to talk to Elaine's or Mike's ex. I have tried to keep good relationships with the parents of the children's exes, the other grandparents, and to make it clear that we are not competitive grandparents.

'It is when they are under 12 that you are important as a grandparent.'

'It is tricky finding a way to give Elaine's children in Cambridge the extra attention we want to give them. But we make the effort. We offer practical support. We go up every three to four weeks now, but last winter we were there every Saturday morning, first thing, when it is freezing-cold here, dark and icy on the roads, so the driving is hard. It is an effort to get up very early after a week of teaching, and go up there to the soccer matches. The three children all play now. Phil was coaching and refereeing. Sometimes the ex took one kid to one game, Elaine took another, and Phil the third to their game, and I went to Elaine's house and did her washing and ironing. She was exhausted, in her first year of being an early childhood teacher, and was finding it emotionally and physically draining. I got the lunch ready for after soccer. We bought her a dryer for her birthday, because she was having difficulty getting clothing dry.

'The kids come to us for holidays. Over Christmas we had them for a fortnight. They'll be here again at Easter. We always build a treasure hunt around the section and up the paddocks, with Easter eggs. The children go to after-school care, and they were going to holiday programmes most of last year. They hated it. They got sick in September. They just needed a break. I said we'd take them. Elaine said, "No, Mum, it's too much for you, with your leukaemia." '

'Leukaemia?' I asked Glenda.

'It is chronic, not acute. I just take my chemo pills every day. I do get tired in the afternoons. Phil is 14 months after a triple-bypass operation, but he's pretty fit now. We said, "No, it's not a problem." We'd done this before with Caitlin and Leo during Mike's family's troubled times. And even now we always have that family for a week when they come back from Doha for holidays. So we took Elaine's children and gave them some attention and a break.'

'What did you do?'

'I did the meals, washing and ironing, and Phil did all the active stuff. He's a brilliant grandad.'

I coaxed more information out of Glenda.

'We took them up the mountain. We picnicked at Lake Rotoaira. We visited the Aquatic Centre at Turangi — three times. We went to the trout hatchery. We played mini-golf. We read to them. We had all the board games out. I taught Flynn to vacuum: he wasn't efficient, but he got the idea. We made and ate burgers. I made them all go-to-bed soft toys. I nearly gave myself repetitive strain injury! I guess we just kept them busy and happy. They do love coming down here.'

'I bet.'

'And we have managed to go to Brisbane about once a year. Oliver was born three weeks early, when Elaine's children were staying with us. We were all driving home from Turangi one day when we got the phone call. I went over after Oliver was born, with Elaine. It was in term time. I could only go for a weekend that first time. That was hard. I wanted to be more help.

'But for Donna and Mike, this is their last year in Doha. They want to go to the Gold Coast so they will be near Lauren and Dan. I find it hard, them all being so far away, but I am incredibly glad we had Leo and Caitlin in their early years and we did as much as we did for them.

It's the early memories that children have that are the important ones. When they are teenagers their focus is on their peer group, not their grandparents! It is when they are under 12 that you are important as a grandparent. That is why we make the most of the time we have with the three in Cambridge. And why we want to go and see more of little Oliver in Queensland.'

Phil came in, and Glenda sat back and continued her knitting. She knits for all the grandchildren, dolls' clothes, scarves, soft toys. 'I made an outfit for Rupert Bear. I had to overstitch the vertical lines in his trousers. It took a bit of doing.' She's in the process of making cat, frog, fox and bear scarves. While I was there she was working on the frog one. I was astonished by how long it was.

The email pinged. It was Lauren commissioning her mother to knit a light jacket for Oliver for the Queensland winter.

Phil Burkett

The Grandad loft

Phil added to the list of things the children did when they visited.

'I took them on the miniature train at our local marae. It's 25 minutes around the track. The kids love playing in the big garden. It's special for the Doha ones: they are stuck indoors over there because it's too hot in summer. They run up and down our hill. We had a big slip-and-slide in the back garden. They love Hide and Seek in the grass and the trees and the sheds. We set up badminton on the back lawn.

'Brothers Harry and Flynn had a go at each other with Star Wars light sabres. I tried to improve their soccer skills. I swam with them. (Glenda can't because of psoriasis.) We've got these big boxes of Lego we've accumulated, so we made Lego towers and creations.'

Glenda suggested I might like to see the loft. Phil took me outside, into a huge shed. Michael's motorbike was there, waiting for him to return from Doha. I registered that grandparents' sheds do tend to become storage units for their children's stuff.

We climbed to a large loft room with two single beds. 'The grandkids are old enough now to sleep up here. It's a treat.'

I saw that it was indeed a treat. All of the walls bristled with shelves. All of the shelves were full of toy soldiers and models of aircraft, ships, tents, helicopters, tanks, jeeps, trucks, landing craft — anything. Most were made of paper or cardboard boxes or tubes, and Sellotape and paint.

'Sellotape doesn't last forever. Polyurethane spray helps it to last a bit longer. My first model is here — I made it when I was 14 years old. It's meant to be a Rolls-Royce armoured car from World War Two in the desert campaign. Restoration work is needed. It's a matter of getting the time.

'This one,' said Phil, 'is made of paper, so it's a bit flimsy. I do this on long winter evenings. It's just a bit of fun. They're all joined together with pins, glue, Sellotape. They don't last. That one's 23 years old, but it's starting to come apart. It has a mini motor inside it, then the fairing goes inside.

'Harry wanted to know about Anzac Day for school. He is named after Glenda's father, who was at Gallipoli, one of the Anzacs. Elaine got him to ring me and talk about the battles over the phone, but the phone isn't really ideal for a kid to see what was actually happening, so I thought I'd put it in context more and I made these maps, plans of different battles, and I made up this game. I took the kids to the Army Museum at Waiouru. They had fun dressing up at the Quartermaster's Store there. When we came home I showed them the maps, and we really got into the games. Here's the Gallipoli trench, Gallipoli landing — these are the contour lines. You have to get all of your men on these slots. You throw the dice and get different moves with different numbers. I've put a time limit on your turn: five minutes. If you throw a three, you can come out of this trench.

'We took the collection of soldiers down to the lounge, and Harry and I re-fought Operation Overlord from World War Two. This is a map of the Normandy coast. This is the Normandy landings. It's set up so that the Brits will win, because they did, eventually. Flynn is only six, but he understands it. Harry, eight, totally understands it.

'You never know until further down the track what impact you have. You just do your best and hope.'

'That's a troop-carrying helicopter there. I'm trying to get the doors to open and close properly. It's just an old Kleenex box. I haven't put the motors in it yet. All-up cost? Nine dollars for the motor. The Thunderbolt plane over here isn't finished yet, but it does go. It's a fan.

'I didn't grow up with computers. I grew up being sporty. When we couldn't go outside when the weather was bad, we made things. We had no money, so I made do with what I had — cardboard. I like to show the grandkids these things, to show them what is possible with not very much: cardboard, pencils, paint.'

I asked Phil if he thought playing with the grandkids has helped them resolve difficulties they have had with the marriage break-ups.

'You never know until further down the track what impact you have. You can't tell. You just do your best and hope. I hope that the kids get a sense of fun from making things to play with. You don't have to sit around doing nothing, just staring at a TV or iPad. When we went to Cambridge last time, the kids had started making Star Wars battle games for themselves with Lego pieces.'

♥

Polly Sussex

A varied crop of grandchildren

I sipped Earl Grey tea with Polly Sussex in her apartment in Albany, then carefully placed the cup on the table, making sure I didn't put it on any of the manuscript music scattered in drifts. She's editing tracks of solo cello performance with harpsichord. We'd just been on the balcony admiring the striped tomatoes she's growing in pots. Polly is the only viola da gamba performer in Auckland. She plays cello as well, seventeenth- and eighteenth-century music mostly. She plays in a chamber group, Affetto, and tours the country. She was telling me about her PhD on Boccherini, the eighteenth-century composer.

'I love playing from copies of music with original notation that is only used by lute and viol players. At the moment the research is on the back-burner because the grandchildren need time. When they are all at school, I might get back to doing research. I might, but there's a third one on the way now. Not a third eighteenth-century composition to transcribe; no. A third grandchild.'

Polly has two daughters. One, Nicola, has a Cambodian Chinese husband and two children, Jade and Marcus. The other has married a man from Borneo who has an Indian dad and a mother from the Dusun tribe of Borneo. They are expecting their first child. 'When we were children, we thought that of course we must be tolerant of different ethnicities, but it was theory; intermarriage wouldn't have been the norm, as it is now in New Zealand. It's a very good thing when it is your own children who give you this opportunity, because it becomes a natural part of your life.

'I think the part-Indian/Malay child yet to be born will have the opportunity to see two completely different cultures, one from South-East Asia and one from here. When I went to the wedding in Borneo, I had to wear the traditional dress of the Dusun tribe and dance a traditional dance with the other women in the group. And then we ate goat curry. It was wonderful to be a part of that. The parents grow pineapples in Borneo. They have five children, all married to Kiwis.

'In the other family, my Chinese Cambodian son-in-law came here when he was four, from a refugee camp in Thailand. He's never been to Cambodia. He cooks Cambodian food, learnt from his mother. He spoke a dialect of Cambodian with his mother, and apart from that he knows a small amount of Mandarin. But because his parents were trying to overcome their experience of the Pol Pot regime, which damaged their lives so much, they didn't talk about their past, so he has no knowledge of it. Jade's Chinese Cambodian grandfather lives in Dunedin. When his wife died it left a terrible deep hole, and because he is so traumatised by Pol Pot he stays in his room all day. He doesn't speak English.

'Even my elder daughter isn't the Kiwi she seems. She has a British passport because she was born in London. I'd like my grandchildren to connect with their many cultural heritages. This kind of intermarriage gives an opportunity to spread peace and co-operation and understanding of other cultures. I'm pleased to be on the fringes of this. It has taught me so much to look at other people and see how they live. In the future we will all end up intermarried.

'The downside of this is that my ex-husband and myself and my partner are the only easily accessible grandparents. I am the local on-call grandmother. My ex-husband is in London for six months, so it's the old story. "Go to Mum first. She'll be more reliable." '

I asked Polly if it was difficult to decide to put aside time from her busy life to look after the grandchildren.

'No. Following the break-up of my marriage — which was *my* doing — I had a difficult relationship with my daughter for at least 10 years, lasting into her adulthood, and I feel a sense of duty to give her back something I had robbed her of earlier on. I wasn't there when she was a teenager, basically. The relationship was so damaged. So it wasn't difficult, because I felt now I could give something to prove that I really did care. She needed the help. They couldn't have afforded a house if they had to pay daycare as well as the mortgage. They could afford only three days' daycare. So I said, "I'll do the other two days." My daughter was going to ask the neighbour, who already had two children at home, but I thought it would be better if I did it, because I wouldn't have distractions. I could devote myself to just doing that job. I sometimes do some emailing, but generally I devote myself to doing what the children want to do. Usually I look after them at their house. Sometimes I bring them over here. But I have found that since Marcus arrived — he's now one, and at daycare for three days a week — I do find I'm reluctant to put both grandchildren in a car and drive somewhere. I am more acutely aware of accidents than I've ever been. I prefer to take them on the bus. They think that is a great adventure.

'We take bus trips to Browns Bay, to the library and the playground. And four-year-old Jade loves sushi, so we go out for sushi. We feed ducks. We went to Kelly Tarlton's. We like the productions at The Pumphouse. They have lots of singing-along and lots of visually interesting things. You can feed the swans there. We have a pass to the zoo. We go there to see the "falamingoes". We crawl through the meerkat tunnels. This is very hard on a grandparent's knees.

'When we go to the library, we read half a dozen books while the baby plays with the various toys they have there. Jade decided this so that we don't incur any overdue fines. She's very responsible. We ride scooters and bikes around the deck. We wander in the garden, and go to the beach a lot. In the summertime there is a lot of ducking in and out of the water. When we play memory games with cards, Jade beats all the adults. I can't claim to be the grandma who's always got a full biscuit tin and cakes. That's okay — my daughters and sons-in-law are all good at cooking.

'A lot of the detail of what I did with my own children I can't remember, but the instincts about what to do are still there. You know you have to be looking behind you and around you constantly when there's a toddler there. You don't forget that. You know how brief their attention span is. You know the danger of the swing knocking you in the lip.

'I potter around in the kitchen and just see what Jade is going to do. Sometimes she wants to do a role-play thing. I have the mermaid toy in my hand, and she has another toy and they have a conversation. I was a little surprised by my reluctance to do it in the first place. Then I thought, "I must participate. You can do this. Grandma, come on!" So we do it. I'm always thankful when the role-play games go on at the other end of the lounge, and I can sit down and just hear the mumbled chit-chat as she talks with her toys.

'I like this preschool period, because we grandparents are so influential. I think four is a charming age. Jade seems to be interested in concepts, like love. I find I can discuss quite adult ideas with her. I am painfully aware of grammar. She has picked up "me and Lucy go to the shops". I try to correct her, then I find her father is saying the same thing. No one knows grammar these days.'

I asked if she was teaching them music.

'Singing is good for putting children to sleep. I sing all the old nursery rhymes. I refuse to buy into the theme songs from Disney movies. They get that anyway. I don't disapprove of it. They just don't need to get that from me. I've played my instrument in the living room for Jade to look at and try out. But I haven't done a lot of that, because I want her to come to that herself. As a teacher of music I see so many children whose parents thinks it's a good idea for them to learn, but the drive doesn't come from the child. Then you always end up with this sad situation, when the child is put off and doesn't want to learn anymore because it wasn't their idea in the first place. So when Jade comes here, I play nursery rhymes on the piano and we sing. And what I do love to do is get CDs from the library and we dance and sing. We had a wonderful one recently, South American music, all about numbers. There were number songs, times tables, number sequences, all very catchy and easy to remember. She knows I'm often away rehearsing for concerts, so she knows that is what my life is about. My attitude is: leave instruction until the child decides for themselves they want to be involved with music. Your expectations can be too high with your own children.

'I will be able to look after three grandchildren, when the new baby is born. When I had three children to look after, my husband was away for long periods. You just cope.

'Part of my desire to be involved is because my parents weren't involved much when I had young children. I didn't have a ready grandparent babysitter. My parents were in Australia. For me it was a solo effort, and I know how hard that is. I didn't want that for my daughters. I didn't resent it, but I think it contributed to the break-up of my marriage, because I had been brought up in a household where we children were all spaced far apart. My brother was six years older and my sister six years younger than I, so we all lived in our own worlds, creating our own things. I had to give up playing the cello for a number of years while I was bringing up the children, and my PhD took me 10 years, because I was writing it when my first child was born and correcting it when my third child was born. All of the time I was trying to get bits of it done while they were asleep. There were times I felt I was never going to get back to it, that my creative life had died. That was an enormous frustration, because I came from a family where the arts were a daily focus. The arts were my daily food.

'But now I don't feel grandchildren prevent my being creative. I use

'I am more acutely aware of accidents than I've ever been.'

my time far better than I used to. I think we all use our time better when we are older. You know exactly what you can do in 55 minutes, and how not to waste any of it. I used to be courteous to people who rang up trying to sell things. Now I just tell them not to waste my time, and I put the phone down. It's important, as you get older, to value your time. I feel more capable now of switching within a short period of time from one thing to something else totally different.

'But I do get tired. I always take my instruments with me to work, so if a pupil at the school where I teach is sick, I will spend half an hour practising. If I have a concert coming up, I'll spend the evening practising. Because I have got this space here that is my own, I can practise in the weekend. When I have just Marcus to look after, rather than two, it is easier, because I can practise when the little one is asleep, and he sleeps for two glorious hours. I squeeze a practice in. The practising is invigorating, and refreshes me. The most tiring thing is the teaching. But the teaching is what earns me enough money to live on. I have talented kids to teach, although there are always those who are reluctant learners. In total I see 40 children over a six-day week. It has to be flexible times to fit around everyone's needs, including the grandchildren's.

'There is no conflict with daughters and their husbands about how we do things with the children. We all have the same values. I don't find it necessary to disapprove of anything. If the child is loved and knows what is right and wrong, and cares about other people, it will all turn out fine in the wash.

'I don't think worrying about the future is productive. I'm not inclined to worry. I'm positive. I need to project that if I am to be a good teacher, and a good grandmother.'

We walked out onto the balcony. 'I never get days to blob. I don't blob. I'm not that kind of person. For me, blobbing is sitting down with a book or looking after the heritage tomatoes I grow on the balcony. Look at them! They are all so different. I love the stripy ones. I love the variety.'

♡

Shona Davidson

Making real Kiwi grandchildren

'My son, Wayne, and his wife, Ang, adopted three sibling girls from Utena, a small village 80 kilometres from Vilnius, in Lithuania. It was a four-year process. They were nine, eight and five when they arrived here in Tauranga. The parents introduced them gradually to the rellies. The day Wayne rang me up to invite me to meet them, I had my other granddaughter, four-year-old Sammy, with me. She's the daughter of my other son, Blair, and his wife, Tara. So Sammy and I went over to meet my new granddaughters and Sammy's new cousins. There they were, these three little girls, Viginija, Indrea and Monika, looking up at this strange lady. Ang explained to them — in her basic Lithuanian — that I am their grandmother. They didn't understand. Ang had a translation book with the Lithuanian names underneath pictures. A grey little old lady illustrated "grandmother"! Ang pointed to the picture and they understood. Their faces lit up just like that.

'Being so close to Sammy, who was my only grandchild then, I had worried about how I would bond with them, but it was easy! I just fell in love. We hugged, and we started the process of bonding. They were so small that I could pick them all up together. Even now they are still light enough for me to pick them up and give them a cuddle. It was hardest for Indrea, the middle one. She had been the "mother" of the siblings in Lithuania, the responsible one. Now, of course, she's fine.

'Wayne and Ang brought them to New Zealand just two weeks before school ended, which was perfect, because they were given buddy children at school who looked after them. Over the holidays, in the cul de sac they live in, in Papamoa, all of the children in the street played together all of the time. Everyone wanted to be their friends, because they were such a novelty. Wayne and Ang went from being the only couple on the street with no kids to having kids everywhere. Wayne had set up the garage as a rumpus room. He went in there one day and found seven kids, not one of whom was one of his daughters — they were playing down the street with other children!

'Wayne and Ang got so tired in those first months. It was such a change in their lives. Before the girls, I had thought they were "professionals" and probably wouldn't want children; I was wrong. To help them have some time off, I did lots of babysitting. My first babysitting time was a disaster. The girls had a huge bubble bath before bed. All three of them were in the bath together. They loved it, until they stood up to get out. They were fooling around and Indrea slipped, and cut her chin open on the end of the bath! I managed to press the wound together to stop it bleeding. I had to make that dreaded call to the parents to come home — I felt terrible. When they got home, there were the four of us, three bubbly girls and me, on the sofa. Ang took Indrea off to the doctor. Wayne stayed home and comforted her sisters and me! He tried to make me not feel bad.

'I took the girls for walks along the beach. A beach was never a part of their lives in inland Europe. On the walk they'd all go, "Nanny, we go up." And we'd go up — to the ice cream shop. It's a proper Kiwi ice cream shop with the scoops of ice cream and the cones. Nanny bought them a cone each (although Monika had a tub at first). They never had it in Lithuania. We still do this; they can make the cone last until they get home.

'The first time I collected them from school — they were still all at primary school — I got there and it was chaos. Mothers were yelling at kids, Indrea was yelling at me about a bag of clothes I was meant to have but didn't, someone was coming on a play-date. Another one was going somewhere else for a play-date! Eventually I got that all sorted out, but I told Wayne after that that I'd look after my grandchildren but not other people's children. It's too much. So we decided that Wednesdays would be just Nanny's night, and it has been ever since.

'I have them every Wednesday afternoon, even in the holidays. Even this year, now that Ang isn't working, I still have Wednesday nights for my granddaughters. In the holidays I make sure they have their walking shoes with them, because we have wonderful parks and tracks around here to go walking. Now they are into swimming. When I pick them up from school I take them to swimming lessons. I always have a packed lunch ready for them.

'Last year when Ang was busy with work, I'd cook tea for them, too, or Wayne would have it in the slow-cooker. Now the eldest is 14, so the girls peel the potatoes and set the table. They water the garden. Without being asked, they do the dishes. They do their homework. I learn from their homework. Even at my age things can suddenly click, and I understand something I never understood at school! I enjoy all their subjects. And it isn't just homework I'm learning. They introduce me to all this modern music. They keep us young. Even now, if they stay over with me, they still hop into bed with me in the morning. We chat. That's the bit I love. They might read their books. They're more likely to read to me than me to them.

'They have become Kiwi kids, living by the beach, wearing jandals or sneakers, shorts or trousers. Ang had a struggle to get them all in dresses for my mother's funeral. Monika likes boys' toys and boys' clothes, too. One of them did a triathlon last weekend. They play soccer and basketball. I drive over on Saturday mornings, because we need three cars for their three different sports fixtures.

'They come on holidays with us and go fishing in Dave's boat. He loves trout fishing on Lake Tarawera. Fishing can be boring for kids, so we mix up the outdoor experiences. Last year we took the boat out, went to Hot Water Beach, then came back to the jetty and explored around. Bush Pools are also great hot pools, and out from there they were jumping off the boat and swimming in the hot pools. A guy at Bush Pools said he caught a trout at Red Beach, so, late in the day, we went to Red Beach and Viginija had Dave's rod. She yelled, "Nanny, there's something wrong with this rod!" She couldn't handle it all of a sudden. A fish was on it. Wayne took over the steering wheel, and Dave came over to help her land the trout. You should have seen the excitement! A couple of weeks ago, the line goes *whhhhoooosh* again — and Monika caught one! Indrea has to catch one now ...

'In 2014, we visited London and Lithuania. The girls had been with us five years by then. Eight of us went: Wayne, Ang, the three girls, me, and Ang's parents, the other grandparents. We went to London first, so the girls could meet their [birth] aunt

'I learn from their homework. Even at my age things can suddenly click, and I understand something I never understood at school!'

and uncle and 17-year-old cousin who live there. Wayne and Ang and the girls had kept in contact with them. The aunt and uncle gave each of the girls a photo album that must have been put together by their mother. They contain pictures of the girls as babies and toddlers. They even include the baby scans. The girls treasure these books. It shows how precious it is for them to know their family background. The children know who and where their aunty and uncle are, and they might well join them when they are grown. When we had to leave them, Ang's mother reassured Andreas, the uncle, that his nieces were truly loved,

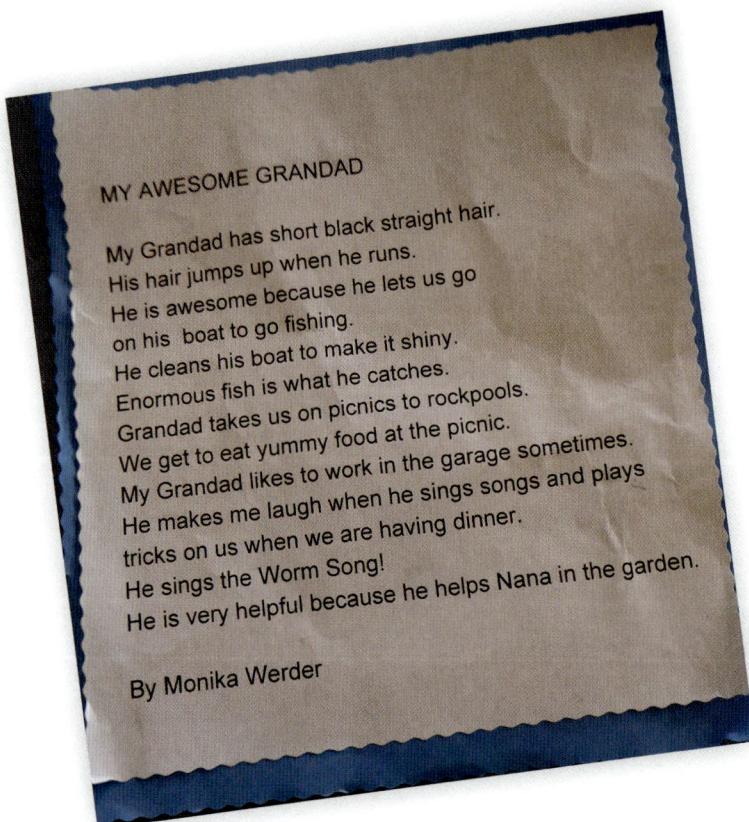

MY AWESOME GRANDAD

My Grandad has short black straight hair.
His hair jumps up when he runs.
He is awesome because he lets us go
on his boat to go fishing.
He cleans his boat to make it shiny.
Enormous fish is what he catches.
Grandad takes us on picnics to rockpools.
We get to eat yummy food at the picnic.
My Grandad likes to work in the garage sometimes.
He makes me laugh when he sings songs and plays
tricks on us when we are having dinner.
He sings the Worm Song!
He is very helpful because he helps Nana in the garden.

By Monika Werder

and he said he could see it. He knew it was all for the best, but it was still so terribly sad for them.

'In Lithuania we stayed in Vilnius, the capital. The woman who organises the adoptions is a most beautiful person. She told us she cries whenever one of the children leaves; they go all over the world. People send her pictures of their children, and she's got this big noticeboard covered in all these smiling faces. She remembers every single child. She's so happy for them.

'We drove out to the village of Utena, where the orphanage was. This was such an eye-opener for me. The village was so poor. The girls had been put in the orphanage by their parents early in their lives, because the parents had addiction problems and couldn't look after them. The girls have photos of their parents on their bedroom walls, so they know what's happened. When they are grown-up I expect the girls will go back to Lithuania and maybe find their parents. The purpose of our visit this time was as a cultural experience for the girls so they could see where they'd come from. They wanted to re-enact some of the original photos they had taken when Wayne and Ang first went there, like one on an old swing. But the swing wasn't there, it was bitterly cold, and the orphanage is now a mission for alcoholics. We did go in; we played a game of basketball there! Then we went to the brand-new orphanage — the people are very proud of it. As well as being for children, it is a refuge for unmarried mothers.

'The girls remember being fond of the orphanage staff, and the staff were delighted to see them after five years. The person who took us around the village was the social worker for the girls previously. He took us to his very modest, small house. All of us had lunch with him and with a couple of teachers from the school. Indrea especially found it intense. Her ex-school teacher, Diana, had arranged for some of her ex-classmates to meet her at the school. The three girls seemed to have forgotten how to speak Lithuanian — they remembered names of food — but everyone is taught English at the school.

'They forget their language so quickly when they are children, because they don't want to be different at school, but also because they only have a child's knowledge of the language, and as they grow up here the language they have a more mature grasp of is English. For a while, Indrea was learning Lithuanian through Skype with someone in Auckland. Ang learnt from her, too.

'Back home, there was a new baby cousin, James, to welcome into the family. Viginija just loves him. She bathed him, fed him, dressed him.

'Adopting the girls has been a win for everybody. I am so aware how unfair the world is, how great the differences between rich and poor countries, how lucky we are here. I am so happy seeing my son, Wayne, being such a good father. I enjoy the unconditional love the girls give me. For us all, it is a splendidly happy time. It makes no difference at all that three of my five grandchildren are adopted. No difference. I adore them all!'

Photo by Derek Onley

Rosemary Penwarden

Protesting for a future

I asked: What was a 57-year-old grandmother from Dunedin doing blocking a third floor corridor in Sky City?

'I'm part of a group called Oil Free Otago. We were blocking the international oil delegates who had come to New Zealand for the 2016 Petroleum Conference. Energy Minister Simon Bridges will be telling them: "These bits of New Zealand are for sale. Come and explore and get more oil and gas here." We wanted to make a statement that we shouldn't drill for more, or even burn what we already have, because, according to the science, there will not be a future for our grandchildren if we do. Having a grandchild makes me think of the future.

'I got into the building with a team of older people. Everyone was staunch and ready to do whatever it took. In front of us were the delegates who couldn't get past us. We sat there, linked arms, and sang a song about a great-granddaughter. It came from the Occupy movement and was sung at the climate talks in Paris.

> People gonna rise like the water.
> We're gonna calm this crisis down.
> I hear the voice of my great-granddaughter
> Saying, "Climate action now."

I have bruises under my arms because I chose to be dragged away. I said to the cops, "You be gentle with me, won't you, because I'm not very strong, but I'm not going to stand up, so you will have to drag me." They were as gentle as they could be. They took us away, processed us, and said that they would arrest us if we came back inside. There were no arrests. There was, instead, communication.'

I asked Rosemary about her own grandchild.

'Arani, my daughter, was taking antibiotics so the Pill wasn't working. She was in a new relationship, and unexpectedly pregnant. They debated about whether they should abort or not, and they involved me in the debate. I was the first person she rang when she knew she was pregnant. She was just finishing her degree. The following day was her last exam. I said, "Put this aside today and do your exam tomorrow, and then we'll talk about it." They were expecting me to be the older, wiser person here. I felt that responsibility. I wanted to be very careful to not put my views. I had had an abortion once, just before I took off overseas. I didn't want them to feel bad if they decided differently from me. I let them talk and I asked questions. I told them I would support them, either way.

'I was at Arlo's birth. They told me they wanted me there. It was a difficult birth, without medical intervention. It was one of the hardest things I've experienced, seeing my daughter in such pain and not being able to fix it for her. She was brave. I was the one taking the rescue remedy! The moment he slipped out and they put him on her tummy — that was it for me. I have been in love with him ever since.

'I was working part-time then, working from home, on contract, writing magazine articles for trade unions. I've deliberately arranged my life so I have time to do the things I think are important. Arlo became one of those things I think is important. I spent as much time as I could supporting them. When he was very little, she would sometimes leave him with me overnight, expressing milk. This was amazing to me, because I could never have left my babies at all. It wasn't the same for her. She left him with his paternal grandfather, too. He looks after him as often as he can as well. In fact, we almost fought over him! "I'm having him." "No, *I'm* having him."

'I was really busy with climate change work and trying to earn a bit of money via the union contract. But if they asked me to have Arlo, yes, I would do it. Everything else was put aside. Jeanette Fitzsimons came to Dunedin and talked about Solid Energy digging up the Mataura Valley. This would increase our national carbon emissions by up to 20 per cent. She said she was going to spend the rest of her life fighting it. Something went *ping* in my chest. I thought, "Oh no! I am going to be doing this by her side." Arani went back to studying again when Arlo was two and a half, and I then made time for a regular day a week, my day, with Arlo.'

'How do you see his future?'

'Bob Lloyd, a physicist, says it will probably be 2030–2034 that we hit 2 degrees of global warming. By 2034, Arlo will be only in his twenties. I'm trying to prepare him to cope with that. My job is to keep him grounded, to make him practically and physically capable of understanding the world around him. I want him to learn to communicate well with people, to be able to negotiate, to be able to say what is important. In our homes now, we have almost forgotten how to communicate. I've been in Third World countries and seen that they are better communicators because they have to negotiate everything regarding their survival. And I want him to have practical skills.

'I now feel like my job is to teach. I am going to work to make Arlo's future the least bad I can. I know we are way past having the world we grew up in. He has to be equipped for the scary future. Now I have the reason, the biggest reason, to fight for the future. It's personal, but it is also for all children.

'My partner, Derek, and I bought a piece of land, 12 acres, a year ago. It is for the future generations, not for us. It is land for growing local food for this community. Some young people in the climate-change movement are saying they won't have children. They are giving up so much for their beliefs. I want this land to be for those people, too, for everyone to grow food. It's a place where Arlo could live in the future, a wee lifeboat. My plan is to build a small dwelling, maybe mudbrick, for him. We've sat together on the hillside and talked. "This will be the bedroom, this the kitchen," we say to each other.

'We have an orchard and he has planted his own pear tree this year, for his fourth birthday, and it is already taller than him. He's helped plant the whole orchard. He carries the sacks, the water; he pats the dirt, puts the rabbit-proof baskets over the seedlings. He's seen a dead possum. We've had lots of discussion about that. He watched it being buried with an apple tree on top.

'We can spend the day somewhere in his imagination.'

'When he was a bit younger, he and I would spend the day somewhere, anywhere, in his imagination, maybe Mars or the Asteroid Belt. Now I'm feeling I want to bring him back to reality. I want him to know about the world, in a nice way. We were talking about pipes one day. We went outside and traced the pipes, where they were, where they joined together, how it all worked. He was fascinated. We look at the hot-water cylinder, and figure out how that works. We plant trees, vegetables, flowers. We hunt for wild strawberries. We watch the birds and we name them. We feed the chooks. We grind up the shells to give to them. We collect their eggs, clean the nests. He can name the herbs and flowers as we walk down to the chook house — forget-me-nots, calendula, thyme. The things you can eat, the things you can't eat. The mint, the chickweed and the dock. If he gets a bee-sting he knows which leaf will help him. He knows the smell of fresh tomatoes in the greenhouse. He knows the sting of stinging nettles, and touching the wrong thing. He knows about prickles in the toe, because he didn't want to put his shoes on. The taste of bitter rocket and sweet baby carrots that he's dug up himself, maybe even planted himself.

'I always like to make sure there is something ordinary that he can do, that we are busy with, when he is here. He loves doing jobs. I always tell him he's a great helper. He empties my dishwasher. He knows where everything goes. He helps wash the clothes. I don't buy him things. I can't bring myself to buy him crap. We use old cardboard boxes. His other grandparents buy him lots of toys. His other grandfather has a TV, and when Arlo was three he asked me where our TV was. I told him we didn't have one. "That's not fair," he said. I keep him away from a screen as much as I can. He knows where his games are on the iPad that his mother has, but I don't do that.

'Derek is different from me. He doesn't want to hear about the latest science predictions or emissions. He knows things are bad. He wants to focus on the solutions, not the dire warnings. He plants trees. It keeps him functioning without falling into depression. Arlo's first name for Derek was "hat", because he is always outside and always wearing a hat. They play music together. Derek is a fabulous guitar player.

'My remedy for depression and despair is the demonstrating that I do and the positive people I meet through that, and Arlo, of course. Arlo has taught me to be fully present, in the moment. As he grows, I am re-learning to be clear, to be honest, to speak and act with deliberation. Being a grandmother adds to my purpose, adds to my feeling of responsibility. It has forced me to finally grow up and be the older, wise woman I never thought I could be.'

♡

Paula and John Stevens

❧

Making a home for them

John Stevens is a builder, married to Paula for 50 years. For relaxation they go motor-homing, leaving their house in the care of their son, Daniel, who is in his forties, and his son, Toby, age nine.

Paula was brought up strictly in the Dalmatian community in Dargaville. She left Dargaville when she was nine, in 1955. Her father had put a bet on two horses and won big. They moved to Auckland and bought the Clare Inn on Dominion Road. It was a fish shop. It meant hard work.

What grandparents do

- We listen to our grandchildren.
- We play with them.
- We talk to, and about, them.
- We give them one-to-one attention.
- We cheer from the sidelines and in the school hall.
- We do the school pick-up.
- We arrange family gatherings.
- We bring cousins together.
- Our role evolves; from baby-worshipper to comforter of the older sibling.
- We do housework, cooking, laundry, when required.
- We make finger paint, cards with doilies stuck on them, pinecone birds, pom-poms, pikelets, cupcakes and gingerbread men, and anything out of a cardboard box.
- We make lists.
- We keep drawers full of bottle tops, string, old gift-wrap paper, Sellotape, Blu-Tack, cardboard rolls and glue.
- We stick children's art on the fridge.
- We have picture Band-Aids and Pamol in the first-aid box.
- We nurture monarch butterfly caterpillars and have chrysalises stuck to the lounge walls.

- We never forget a birthday.
- We aim to spread an aura of calm.
- We are strong when something bad happens.
- We don't seek succour; we offer it.
- We know that childhood is fleeting.
- We adore the long eyelashes, the plump knees more like bent pipes than knees.
- We think we are better at child-rearing now, the second time around.
- We are unshockable and tolerant, because of the amount of change our generation has experienced.
- We have long memories.
- We have knowledge of that great stretch of time between remembering our own grandparents' stories, maybe of the Depression, or war, and our valiant, if confused, keeping up with the Xboxes, Minecraft and Tweets of our grandchildren. We have knowledge of at least five generations, spanning more than a century — grandparent, parent, ourselves, our children, grandchildren.
- We are family historians, passing on stories, games, songs and family history.
- We are never in a hurry.
- We push swings or roundabouts, and encourage children down slides.
- We have, or make, time, the best gift we give our grandchildren.

Acknowledgements

Thank-yous

The author gratefully acknowledges the help of all the grandparents interviewed for this book.

She would also like to thank the teachers and children from Owairaka School, Mt Eden Normal School and Hurunui College for their involvement, in particular Susan Whysall, Amanda Griffin and Paul Munnerley.

Big thank-yous, too, to dear friend Virginia Pawsey for help in the South Island.

Especial thanks to Sue, Mary, Anne Marie and Mandy at The Kids Studio, Mt Eden, without whom I wouldn't have had a happy grandchild and some child-free time to write this book.

And thank you to Robert and Mia for the gift of Tane.

Acknowledgements

The author acknowledges, with gratitude, the support of a grant from the Contestable Fund of Copyright Licensing New Zealand.

Photographs are by the author unless credited otherwise.

I gratefully acknowledge the following children for generously allowing me to reproduce their original artwork: Seraphina Whiunui-Vaka (p. 2); Harmony Naeata (p. 16); Amy Everitt (p. 24); Drea Jones (p. 52); Harry Sidey (p. 61); Thea Bond (pp. 62–63); Sydney White-Taumaunu (p. 81); Charlie Beagley (pp. 92–93); Mitchell Cullen (p. 107); Ridha Parkar (p. 137); Callay and Frida Gardiner (p. 147); Eliza Fletcher (p. 155); Dupree Pomare (pp. 174–175); Billy Leaf (p. 202); Arlo Skinner (p. 229); Mariam Yacoub (p. 245).